## EXTRA ACTIVITIES

LONDON, NEW YORK, MUNICH, MELBOURNE, DELHI

*for Barney, Ashleigh, Eden and Brodie
Ed, Amie and Esmé
Daniel, Emily and Imogen*

**Brand Manager for Dr. Miriam Stoppard** Lynne Brown
**Senior Managing Editor** Jemima Dunne
**Editor** Jinny Johnson
**Senior Art Editor** Helen Spencer
**Designer** Carla De Abreu
**DTP Designer** Jackie Plant and Traci Salter
**Production** Sarah Sherlock

**Publishing Director** Corinne Roberts

First published in the United Kingdom in 2005

Published in the United Kingdom by Dorling Kindersley
80 Strand, London WC2R ORL

A Penguin Company

1 3 5 7 9 10 8 6 4 2

Copyright © 2005 Dorling Kindersley Limited
Text copyright © 2005 Miriam Stoppard

A CIP catalogue record of this book is available
from the British Library
ISBN 0756609534

Publisher's note – Material in this book was originally
published as part of the Baby Skills Pack produced in 2000

Colour Reproduction by GRB Editrice
Printed and bound in Singapore by Tien Wah Press

See our complete catalogue at
**www.dk.com**

# Your baby's first year

Your baby's growth and development cover three main areas in her first year

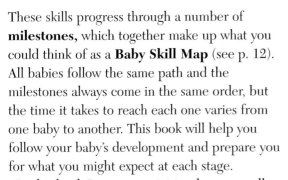

- using her *brain to think* and to develop language
- learning to stand upright and walk, starting with *attempts to control her head* as early as her first week
- acquiring *fine control of her fingers* so that by 10 months she can pick up a pea between her thumb and forefinger.

These skills progress through a number of **milestones,** which together make up what you could think of as a **Baby Skill Map** (see p. 12). All babies follow the same path and the milestones always come in the same order, but the time it takes to reach each one varies from one baby to another. This book will help you follow your baby's development and prepare you for what you might expect at each stage.

In this book I suggest activities that cover all the main areas of development and fit in with *your baby's natural milestones* so that her truly astonishing skills will be acquired in concert with growth of her brain and body. Not *before,* because that would be forcing her, and not *after,* for that would hold her back. Instead, you'll be helping at *just the right time*. And if you follow the **Baby Skill Map** you will avoid falling into the trap of expecting too much too soon. You'll be alert to her emerging skills and be ready to help her move forward as soon as she's ready.

## LET YOUR BABY LEAD YOU

All you have to do to help a skill develop is *take your lead from your baby*. This is the golden and unbreakable rule of child development.

And your baby will always show you with some sign that she wants to and can move on.

It's important to follow her lead because if you do you'll hit exactly the right moment when it's essential for her to acquire the skill.

This makes her feel very pleased with herself (especially if you praise her) and you'll be building her self-confidence and self-esteem right from the start, even when she's only a very young baby. Just think what a confident, balanced, affectionate child she'll grow into. **And all the groundwork is laid in the first year.**

## THE LINKS BETWEEN GROWTH AND THE EMERGENCE OF SKILLS

If you think of the complexity and delicacy of picking up a pea between finger and thumb you'll understand that certain things must happen in your baby's body before she can acquire such manual dexterity. After all she can't pick up a pea at birth. A lot of elements have to come into place first, such as

- muscles that will draw finger and thumb together and grip
- muscles that will obey the brain when it sends the message to grip

• eyes that can see the pea clearly
• co-ordination between what the eye sees (where the pea is, how far it is from the eyes) and where the hand moves (hand-eye co-ordination)
• a brain well enough developed to desire the pea and give the command to the muscles to work
• nerves in place to carry the order from brain to muscle.

All these elements have to be acquired by your baby in nine months – a huge amount of development which has to be successfully orchestrated in all departments before a pea can be retrieved between finger and thumb.

As each phase dawns you can track it. So at two months you can see your baby's desire to grab something, even though she hasn't developed enough to do so – she "grasps with her eyes" (see p. 22). I will help you follow your baby's track with games that encourage her to go on to the next phase.

Understanding this principle that growth and development **must** be in place before a skill can be acquired is very important when later your baby acquires bowel and bladder control, not to your timetable but to her own individual timetable of development. And you can't, nor should you, expect it a moment earlier. Babies can't become dry overnight to order nor can they perform for you when you sit them on a potty. Forcing the issue stores up trouble for the future.

## THINGS TO LOOK OUT FOR

In the early months there are only a few things to concern yourself with. You might think that your baby is
• slow to see
• hard of hearing
• a bit "floppy".
It's easy to test these things yourself.
In the first month
• she'll smile if she sees your face and she can if you're 20-25 cm (8-10 in) away
• she'll turn her eyes and then later her head if she hears a noise – scrunching up tissue paper is a good test so is ringing a little bell
• she should begin to stop her head lolling back when you pull her up from lying with her arms (see p. 15 and Activity 37). If you're doubtful about any of these things talk to your health visitor or doctor.

# DO BOYS AND GIRLS DEVELOP DIFFERENTLY?

Boys and girls are equipped differently at birth and subsequently develop differently. If you're aware of the differences you can concentrate on your baby's strengths and encourage her or him positively in less able areas.

I point out the differences not because they make one gender superior to the other, but to give you insight into how your baby ticks. Understanding boy/girl differences will help you to give time to those aspects of your baby's development that need special attention.

Girls are born with two advantages over boys.

**Language** The verbal centres in the left side of a girl's brain are further along the skill map than boys so anything to do with language is generally acquired earlier in girls.

**Emotional understanding** The two sides of a girl's brain have already developed connections at birth (these connections are not in place in boys till nine months), allowing girl babies to be more comfortable with their emotions and sensitive about the feelings of those around them.

## HOW YOU CAN HELP

Now knowing this, if you have a baby boy (and I had four) you can help them negotiate these potential difficulties.

*Speech*
- Be very verbal – and speak clearly.
- Sing lots of songs.
- Play lots of clapping and action games.
- Play classical music tapes.

*Emotions*
- Give lots of physical contact.
- Emphasize success with praise.
- Deal promptly with anger, fear and frustration.
- Treat boys and girls exactly the same when they need consoling or they cry – it's never right to expect a little boy to suppress his feelings "because he's a boy".

## OTHER DIFFERENCES

- The cortex which determines intellect develops in the womb earlier in girls' brains than in boys'.
- The left half of the cortex which controls thinking develops earlier in girls than in boys.
- The right and left sides of the brain connect to each other earlier and better in girls and this gives them an advantage in reading skills, which draw on both sides.
- From the start boys are better at spatial visualization than girls so girls may need help in working out three-dimensional concepts.
- By school age, boys are usually better than girls at running, jumping and throwing.

# Help your baby learn

Your baby is born with some innate survival instincts. Because every baby has these you can use them to help your baby learn.

- She's born **wired to smile** at faces and can see yours at 20-25 cm (8-10 in) so she'll smile from birth and learn to be friendly and sociable.

- She's **programmed to hear high** sounds and **born to communicate** so talk to her at 20-25 cm (8-10 in) and she'll "mouth" back.

There are a number of quite abstract ideas that we adults take for granted, but that require huge intellectual skills for a baby. The best way to help and encourage your baby's development is through her senses – sight, hearing, touch, smell and taste – because these are what she will be using to explore the world before she can move about independently.

## UNDERSTANDING OPPOSITES

It's hard for a baby to get the hang of what "hot" means if she's presented with the idea on its own. But if you give her the **opposite**, it's much easier for her to understand. So always try to describe a concept such as "hot" in relation to its opposite, "cold".

**Examples of opposites**

textures = **hard and soft**
tastes = **sweet and sour**
edges = **sharp and blunt**
sizes = **big and small**

The reasoning behind this is that babies and children find it quite difficult to understand the differences between things. You can make their job easier by making the differences very plain: differences are at their most obvious with opposites. Demonstrate "hot" (only warm in reality) by letting your baby find something cool to feel immediately after, making sure you use the words **"hot"** then **"cold"** at the same time. Adding actions helps. So blow on your fingers with hot and shiver with cold. (Be careful not to let your baby touch something really hot.)

## RECOGNITION

Babies, like adults, learn by repetition and you'll help her by repeating what I call the "defining features" of something over and over again. This promotes recognition – a very complex intellectual skill. For instance, every time you see a cat you describe its defining features: four legs, whiskers, long tail, fur, pointy ears, says "miaow", can jump up high. The defining features of a bird are feathers, beak, wings, two legs, can fly.

Constantly describing the defining features of something helps to fix it in your baby's mind and helps her distinguish it from the myriad other objects she's seeing for the first time every day. By the time she's about 10 months, she'll know that your *pet cat*, her cuddly *toy cat* and the *picture of a cat* in her book are all cats and she'll also know that your pet is real, but the others are just representations. This is very sophisticated thinking!

## TELLING LIKE FROM UNLIKE

Your baby is able to understand defining features because of her ability to discern **like** from **unlike**. Matching shapes or objects and being able to tell like from unlike is a huge step in intellectual thinking but babies are surprisingly good at it and it develops from a very early age. From as early as 16 weeks she can see the difference between shapes on a card. Try this out with your baby using Activity 9, *Baby brain teaser*. You'll find that your baby can distinguish not only **shape** but **size**.

The next step in telling like from unlike could be a demonstration of the *properties* of three-dimensional shapes. For instance, round blocks **roll**, square ones don't. As soon as you can prop your baby up (about 2-3 months) roll a balloon towards her and say "The balloon's **round** so it **rolls**." Then repeat with a soft square brick: "The brick is square so it can't roll." She won't understand at first, but your constant reinforcement of the idea will eventually help her to fix the differences in her mind.

From this your baby progresses to shapes fitting in holes (see Activity 12, *Bricks and blocks*) and then to easy puzzles. And you can also show her matching and non-matching shapes with ordinary household items such as pans, baking tins or yoghurt pots.

## CUES AND SIGNALS

It's very important never to push your baby, but to go at her pace and encourage her when she lets you know she's ready. Spotting this moment of readiness is not as hard as you think; she'll give you **cues** and **signals** that make her intention clear. For instance

- at about two weeks, your baby will probably try to raise her head a little when lying on her tummy – this is a cue telling you she's ready for the game that strengthens her neck (see Activity 37, *Newborn baby jig*)
- at five months she'll blow raspberries at you to cue you for games where you imitate noises (see Activity 47, *Puff and blow*)
- at nine months she can point so get her to point things out in her books (see Activity 14, *More about books*)
- at around 10 months she'll start pulling herself up to standing – she's getting ready to walk so place furniture so that she can cruise round it (see Activity 19, *Obstacle course*).

## DESCRIBE AND DEMONSTRATE

Babies need descriptions and demonstrations for understanding – they also love a running commentary from you to tell them what you're doing and what's happening. So from the moment your baby's born, start talking and keep talking. If a word or explanation describes an action always demonstrate it. "This flower has a lovely **smell**" (sniff, sniff). "We stroke doggies **gently**" (stroke, stroke). And later, "We close the door **quietly**" (get up and demonstrate). For this reason I've suggested throughout this book that you describe and demonstrate what you do.

This emphasis on talking has another important outcome. It helps your baby learn to speak – the most complex of all human skills. The ability to acquire speech is amazing because it involves bringing together listening to the sounds of speech, being able to repeat those sounds and to recognize the meanings to which the sounds are attached. So talking to your baby is not idle chatter – right from the start it's the key to communication and language skills.

## ACT OUT YOUR EMOTIONS

Babies and children get the message better through actions rather than words alone and this phase lasts till they're six or more. Babies love it if you act out your emotions so make sure you accompany as many words as possible with actions and expressions and **exaggerate** them all – especially pleasure and joy.

So the rule is **be theatrical** whenever possible – larger than life, dramatic, over the top. End everything with giggles, laughter and cuddles whenever you can and make and keep eye contact with your baby as much as possible, especially when she's very young.

## EMOTIONAL CONTINENCE

"Emotional continence" means being able to handle emotions, not letting them get out of hand. It involves being able to control strong emotions by turning them to good purpose.

• Babies learn **emotional continence** from you.

• If **emotional continence** isn't learned in the first year it's very difficult to acquire later. It's important for your baby to acquire emotional continence. Without it she finds it very difficult to cope with anything that thwarts her wishes or stands in her way as she grows up – in other words she becomes emotionally *incontinent*. The classic outcome of emotional incontinence is a pre-schooler who bullies, is disruptive, even destructive at home and at nursery school.

**Building emotional continence**

It's not difficult to impart early lessons in emotional continence to your baby. There are three easy steps in any situation.

• *Legitimize your baby's emotions*. Tell her, "I know it hurts" if she's fallen over or "That is annoying" if she's frustrated by something and becomes angry.

• *Defuse your baby's emotions*. Say, "Mummy will kiss it better" or "Daddy gets annoyed with that too, you know."

• *Move on from the emotion*. Suggest, "When it's stopped hurting we'll go out to play" or "Let's forget that and have a cuddle."

# YES AND NO

Babies start to understand the difference between "Yes" and "No" as early as three months because they soon recognize that "No" means an absence of all the positive things they crave from you – smiles, eye contact, cuddles, joy, love and approval. These are the things that show you care for your baby.

The process of learning **no** is simply understanding the temporary withdrawal of your approval, your baby's most precious possession. Understanding **no** is also the first step in understanding discipline and accepting

**no** is the first step in self-control. A change in the tone of your voice, just a quiet subtle one, can act as a signal of your disapproval; it's all that's necessary. So your voice need only change from a loving voice to a toneless one when you say **no**, for your baby to learn that **no** is negative and can be avoided.

When your baby responds positively reward her with a cuddle. **Yes** should be a nod with much laughing. **Yes** is a celebration and a sign of your approval. Make it easy for your baby to distinguish between **yes** and **no**.

# The Golden Hour of play

It's impossible to over-estimate the **importance of play** to babies and young children – it's the **basis for all learning**. Even a newborn baby benefits from play. Your baby's first and **best playmate is you**, his parents. It's you he responds to most readily and it's with you that he lays the foundations for his secure and happy development. I've devised the **Golden Hour** of play to give you and your baby an hour of structured play **tailored to each month's development**.

## WHAT IS THE GOLDEN HOUR?

The Golden Hour is simply an hour of different kinds of play. The suggested activities and games within the hour cover the major areas of your baby's development so that he goes forward on all fronts like a wave creeping up the shore and no area is neglected.

Occasionally, as with the waves on the shore, one area of your baby's development shoots ahead of the rest. To allow for this, each month of the Golden Hour is divided differently to give more time for activities linked to these developmental spurts.

## HOW THE GOLDEN HOUR HELPS

The main point of the Golden Hour is to give your baby your undivided attention for one hour a day, an hour when you focus completely on him and he feels that he's centre stage. I've designed the Golden Hour of play to make it easy for you to find time for this crucial interaction between you and your baby.

It's bonding for your baby. He broadens his horizons through you. He believes in himself and his ability to progress through you. It's a win/win situation: you enjoy spending time with your baby, your baby learns from you.

## TOYS AND TOOLS

Given the chance a baby will turn any object – even a yoghurt pot – into a toy. But certain toys are particularly helpful in stimulating baby development.
**Mirror** From newborn a small mirror secured in the cot so that your baby can see his own face helps him to focus and to reinforce his inborn response to the human face. Older babies love to look at their own and your reflections in mirrors.
**Mobiles** Even for newborn babies a mobile hung 20-25 cm (8-10 in) above the cot stimulates vision.

**Bricks and blocks** Teach touch, grip and stacking.
**Rattles** The sound a rattle makes stimulates your baby to learn about cause and effect. Once he can grasp it he finds that shake = noise.
**Music and rhymes** Classical music helps maths, logic and speech. Nursery rhymes and clapping games help talking and friendliness.
**Books and stories** Introduce books and tell stories to your baby as early as possible – leave a cloth book in his cot.

## USING THE GOLDEN HOUR

The following pages will help you guide your baby through the five main areas of development month by month. In each section I've suggested games and activities that are particularly good for each area. You'll find two of these at the end of each age section and the rest in number order through the book. The Golden Hour clockface shows roughly how long you might spend on each area. There are also suggestions for toys, but you'll have your own ideas too.

## Be flexible

The Golden Hour is flexible. It's not a prescription. I've arranged it as 60 minutes, but these don't have to run consecutively. You can divide the hour up and fit in 10 minutes or quarter-hour play sessions as it suits you during each day. But your baby will benefit most from sustained periods of play with you rather than a snatched five minutes. You can share the hour between partners and family – say a helpful brother or sister and grandparents. Change the games around between you.

*The numbers featured on each Golden Hour clock refer to games and activities particularly suited to that stage. The numbers shown here are examples of each category.*

## KEY TO THE GOLDEN HOUR

### friendliness
Sometimes called sociability. Babies learn social skills from how you relate to them.

### TALKING
Learning to understand and use language.

### mind
Includes the senses and intellectual development.

### hands
Accurate and fine use of his hands and fingers.

### moving
Control of the head and body, leading to sitting, standing and walking.

11

Your baby's main skills are laid out below to give you some idea of when you can expect each skill to emerge, though the timetable is very flexible. When your baby has acquired a skill she's reached one of her "milestones".

## The Baby Skill Map

| months | 0-1 | 1-2 | 2-3 | 3-4 | 4-5 |
|---|---|---|---|---|---|
| **mind** | | | gets excited at sight of breast or bot... | | |
| | | | looks at own hand | | |
| | | spontaneous smile | | | |
| | listens and is alert | | | | |
| **moving** | | | | supports upper bod... | |
| | | lifts head to 45° | | | |
| | | | blows raspberries and bubble... | | |
| | | | squeals | | |
| **TALKING** | mouths | | | | |
| **hands** | | | | grasps rattle | |
| | | holds hands open | | | |
| | grasps your finger tightly | | | | |
| **friendliness** | | | cries at disapproving tone of your voice | | |
| | jigs whole body when sees you | | | | |

# with your baby

Remember that until one skill is learned she can't go on to the next, so you'll help her if you play games that encourage the emergence of skills at just the right time. My **Golden Hour** of games will ensure this.

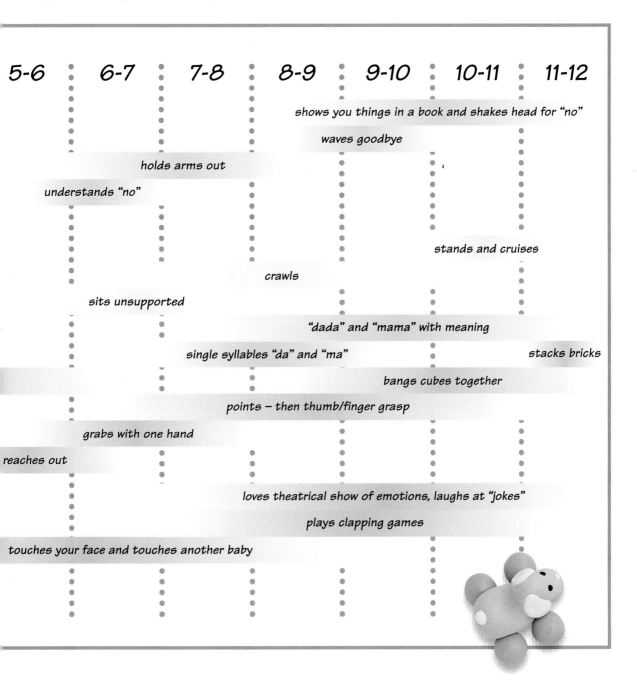

| 5-6 | 6-7 | 7-8 | 8-9 | 9-10 | 10-11 | 11-12 |
|---|---|---|---|---|---|---|

shows you things in a book and shakes head for "no"

waves goodbye

holds arms out

understands "no"

stands and cruises

crawls

sits unsupported

"dada" and "mama" with meaning

single syllables "da" and "ma"

stacks bricks

bangs cubes together

points – then thumb/finger grasp

grabs with one hand

reaches out

loves theatrical show of emotions, laughs at "jokes"

plays clapping games

touches your face and touches another baby

# 0 to 1 month

You're thrilled by the arrival of your new baby, but like most new parents you'll probably feel nervous about handling this tiny scrap of humanity who seems so weak and vulnerable. But in fact, from the moment of birth your newborn

- is a highly developed person with many accomplishments
- is a lot more robust than you think and has a strong instinct to survive.

### Baby skills at birth

*Although your baby is physically helpless at birth he has a number of amazing **innate skills**. Your newborn • is **wired to communicate** • is **programmed to imitate** the facial expressions and sounds you make when you talk • sees everything clearly **20-25 cm (8-10 in)** away and responds eagerly to your face at this distance • at 20-25 cm (8-10 in) can **"read" emotions** and may smile if he sees you smiling • can hear your voice very clearly and recognize it • will "**mouth" back at you** if you talk at a distance of 20-25 cm (8-10 in).*

Congratulations! The long wait is over – your baby is here. But don't be fooled into thinking that all he'll "do" at this stage is sleep and feed…

## *mind*

Your baby **"understands"** from the moment of birth – he's not inanimate. You can chart his progress in the first month. For example

Day 1  He **"stills"** when he hears your voice – he becomes quiet and alert, his body stops moving and he concentrates on listening.

Day 3  He **responds** when spoken to and his gaze becomes intense.

Day 5  At 20-25 cm (8-10 in) he's attracted to things that move so **will watch** your moving lips or your gently fluttering fingers with interest.

Day 9  His **eyes will "dart"** at the sound of a high-pitched voice, indicating he can hear you. He responds better to **high-pitched sounds** than low-pitched ones so instinctive baby talk is good.

Day 14  He can tell you apart from other people.

Day 18  He **turns his head** to sounds.

Day 28  He's learning how to **express** and **control** his emotions and will adjust his behaviour to the sound of your voice: he'll get upset if you speak roughly or loudly and quieten if your voice is soothing.

## NEWBORN REFLEXES

At birth your baby has a set of reflexes that come from his natural instinct to survive. All of these reflexes are lost by the age of three months. They have to be otherwise his development would be delayed and new skills could not emerge.

**Grasp reflex**
Put your fingers against your baby's palms and he'll grasp them so tightly he can take his own weight if you try to lift him gently from lying on his back.

**Rooting reflex**
If you stroke his cheek gently and rhythmically with your finger he'll turn towards your hand and "root around" for the nipple in order to feed.

**Walking or stepping reflex**
He'll make primitive step movements if you hold him upright and let his feet touch a flat surface. He'll step up if you bring the front of his leg in contact with the edge of a table.

**"Moro" response**
If he feels he's falling or if he's startled he'll spread out his arms and legs in a star shape. It's thought that this instinct originates from when our ancestors lived in trees and used this technique to break their fall.

# m°ᵥⁱng

His movements may be limited by his lack of strength at this stage, but from day one your baby is starting to **try out his muscles** and he
• can make small movements and adjust his position – when lying on his tummy he'll **lift** his feet a little and try to **bend** his knees
• will turn his head to a preferred side when he's lying down and when on his tummy he'll try to **lift his head** for a second. This is very difficult for him to do this because his head's too heavy for his back and neck muscles and will be for several weeks yet – your baby's head is relatively large at approximately a quarter of his entire length
• jigs and wriggles and **steps** when held in an upright position
• keeps his legs curled up when he's on his back as he did in the womb
• **jerks** (or "bobs") his head into an upright position when he's nursed on your shoulder.

# hands

It will be a while before your baby realizes his hands are a part of him or that he has any control over them – his fingers remain tightly curled for at least three weeks. Once the grasp reflex (see page 15) is lost, his hands relax and begin to open. Meanwhile he'll hang on to your finger even when he's asleep.

## TALKING

Your baby was born wired for sound and is longing to talk. He's a natural conversationalist.
• From birth he'll **respond** if you speak animatedly to him with your face 20-25 cm (8-10 in) from his by "mouthing" with his lips and tongue, like a fish feeding.
• From two weeks he makes his own **non-specific sounds**.
• From three weeks he has a baby sound **vocabulary**.
• From four weeks he understands the interchange of conversation and knows how to respond when you talk to him. From early on he **leads the conversation** and *you* follow *him*.

## friendliness

Your baby is born friendly and longs for company so he
• wants to respond to you and **listens** and **looks** intently even at birth
• demonstrates this with whole-body jerks, mouthing, sticking out his tongue, nods, bobs, throwing out his hands and spreading his fingers
• **smiles from birth** if he can see you talking and smiling at him from a distance of 20-25 cm (8-10 in) from his face
• loves to have **eye contact** and **skin contact**, especially when he's feeding
• can **show emotions** by using the correct face muscles to smile and grimace – he'll be **upset** if he hears a harsh-sounding voice.

# *The* Golden Hour

For how to use The Golden Hour see pages 10-11

Although your newborn baby mainly feeds and sleeps you can use his wakeful times to promote his innate desire to communicate and play with you.

## "keep talking
to your baby"

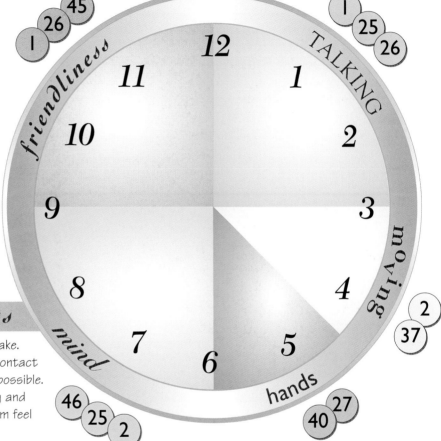

### *friendliness*

**Cuddle** him whenever he's awake. Try to give him skin-to-skin contact with both parents whenever possible. By gently stroking, caressing and massaging him you'll make him feel both loved and secure.

## TALKING

**Start talking** to your baby the instant he's born and never stop. Say his name over and over (and watch his eyes dart in response).

## *mind*

Play your baby some **classical music**. As well as soothing him it will encourage him to listen, make sounds and, believe it or not, add up numbers later.
Suitable prop: **music tape**

## m°v°ing

Gradually **uncurl your baby's limbs** to help him straighten his body. Try baby massage too, as this increases body awareness and makes him stretch.

## hands

**Play** with his hands and fingers to encourage him to open his fists.
Suitable prop: **textured bricks, soft toys**

17

# ① Newborn baby chatter

This isn't just idle chatter! It's the **first step** on your Baby's Skill Map for learning to talk. Talking to your baby with **focused attention** and your face 20-25 cm (8-10 in) from his will encourage an amazing list of emerging baby skills, especially **imitation**, a baby's most **powerful learning tool**. Start the minute he's born.

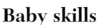

### Baby skills

that will benefit from "Newborn baby chatter":
- *talking and communicating*
- *listening* • *seeing* • *becoming friendly* • *forming relationships*
- *reading your moods*
- *handling emotions*
- *imitation*

## Name game

Cradle your baby in your arms with your face 20-25 cm (8-10 in) from his. Say his name over and over until you attract his attention. Then say, "What a good boy!" several times with warmth and pleasure in your voice.

## Making faces

Cradle your baby and start acting emotions with appropriate facial expressions and explanations. Keep up a running commentary of the emotions your face is expressing: "Mummy's so happy she's laughing" (laugh); "Mummy's puzzled so she's frowning" (frown).

## Eye to eye

Cradle your baby with your face 20-25 cm (8-10 in) from his. Look into his eyes and hold his attention by talking, smiling and bobbing your head gently. He'll start "mouthing" (opening and closing his mouth like a fish) and pushing out his tongue – he's imitating your facial movements and trying to answer you. As soon as you see this response, encourage him enthusiastically and pause for a second to give him the two-way rhythm of conversation. Speak again, encourage again, pause again.

## Look and learn

Prop a mirror on one side of your baby's cot so that he can look at his face. Tape a photograph of you or another family member next to it.

# ② Watch it move

A moving object positioned at 20-25 cm (8-10 in) from your newborn baby's face helps his **visual skills** because he can see it even though he can't yet focus at a distance. If the object moves, and especially if it's shiny, your baby will try to **move his eyes** to keep it in his field of vision. This strengthens his eye muscles, helps him learn to co-ordinate both eyes simultaneously and to **move his head** at the same time.

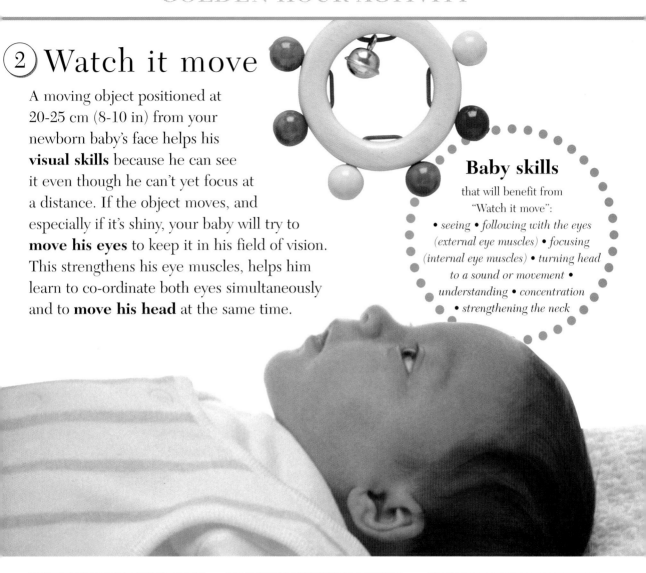

**Baby skills**

that will benefit from "Watch it move":
• seeing • following with the eyes (external eye muscles) • focusing (internal eye muscles) • turning head to a sound or movement • understanding • concentration • strengthening the neck

### Into focus

Hold a shiny mobile or toy on a string 20-25 cm (8-10 in) above your baby's face while he's lying on his back. Bob it gently up and down and call his name. When his eyes fix on the mobile praise him.

### Find the finger

Gently snap your fingertips about 20-25 cm (8-10 in) from his eyes. Place your face in line with your fingertips and call his name. When he notices your fingers praise him and tell him he's a clever boy.

### Follow the finger

Move your snapping fingers slowly to one side and call his name. He'll try to move his eyes to follow your finger. Tell him he's clever! Repeat on the other side.

**0** to **2** months ✓ mind ● talking ✓ moving ● hands ● friendliness

# 1 to 2 months

Although she's still tiny your baby is strengthening physically every day and is becoming a real person. During this month she'll

- gradually lose her newborn reflexes
- begin to show her maturing personality
- start rewarding your affection with spontaneous smiles.

### Eye contact

*New babies adore **cuddles** and thrive on your love and attention. Make **eye contact** with your baby all the time. Turn your body towards her, put your face 20-25 cm (8-10 in) from hers and speak to her in a **sing-song voice**. Bob your head to encourage her to "converse" with you by mouthing at you.*

# During this month your baby stays awake for longer and you'll begin to notice times when she's more alert – that's when she's ready to play and learn.

## hands

Your baby will soon be fascinated by her hands. In preparation for this she
• has completely lost the grasp reflex she was born with by the end of the second month. Her fingers are hardly ever curled in a fist now – they remain wide open most of the time, ready for **clasping** things she wants in her **palm**
• is becoming aware of her **fingers** and she'll begin to **study** them intently by the end of the second month
• has very sensitive fingertips and enjoys having them held, **tickled** and **massaged** by you
• may try to take a swipe at a toy which is held out to her, but she'll miss at this stage – even though her arm movements are by now becoming more purposeful, her ability to judge the distance between the object and her hand (known as her **hand-eye co-ordination)** is still quite poor, as is her muscle control.

## TALKING

As part of her natural desire to communicate with you your baby
• makes **throaty noises** back at you when you speak to her
• has **hearing that's particularly attuned** to the sort of high-pitched, sing-song tone parents, and especially mothers, instinctively adopt when talking to their young babies
• wriggles her whole body in an attempt to **push her tongue out** at you (mouthing) when you speak animatedly to her
• makes simple **vowel sounds** like "eh", "ah", "uh" and "oh"
• will soon **join in** with sounds if you put your face 20-25 cm (8-10 in) from hers and look into her eyes as you chat to her.

## moving

Your baby spends her wakeful moments practising her developing muscle strength. In doing this she
• tries to **lift her head** up and can raise it to an angle of 45° for a second or two when lying on her tummy – a sign that her neck muscles are getting stronger
• can **hold her head** in line with her body for a few moments if you pull her up very gently by her arms when she's lying on her back
• can **hold her head upright** for a few seconds by the end of the second month if you hold her upright with your hands around her chest
• is completely uncurled from the fetal position and her legs can **take the weight of her body** for a second.

## mind

Your baby is taking more of an interest in her surroundings and soon she

• knows who you are and **recognizes you** – she's very interested to see you and shows her excitement by jerking her whole body with pleasure, kicking and waving her legs and arms

• **smiles readily** as soon as her eyes can focus at any distance, usually about six weeks

• **watches what's going on around her** – if she's propped up on cushions or in a bouncing chair, she will **look in the direction** of any sounds and movements

• stares steadily at things that interest her as though she's "**grasping**" them with her eyes.

## friendliness

Your baby is becoming more **sociable** and she

• may stay awake for longer periods after a feed and enjoy watching what you're doing

• can let you know if she doesn't like something or something **upsets** her

• **recognizes** your voice and **gurgles** in response to your conversation

• smiles from a distance as a way of **showing pleasure**

• is a born **mimic** and will observe you closely to imitate you, so be theatrical in all your gestures, show your relationship is based on good humour, kindness, comfort and love

• loves all kinds of **physical affection** so the rule is lots of cuddles at every opportunity.

### Responding to your baby

*When your baby shows she wants you, go to her **holding out your arms**, call her name and let her know you're coming. Gestures such as holding out the arms are **precursors to talking** and although there aren't any words yet, a positive response to her will show her that you understand her.*

"I like lots of...
# cuddles, love, smiles"

# The Golden Hour

Her brain is growing at top speed so the emphasis this month is on the mind. Intellectual development depends on the acquisition of **stereoscopic vision**, when the eyes work together and develop the ability to focus images, however distant.

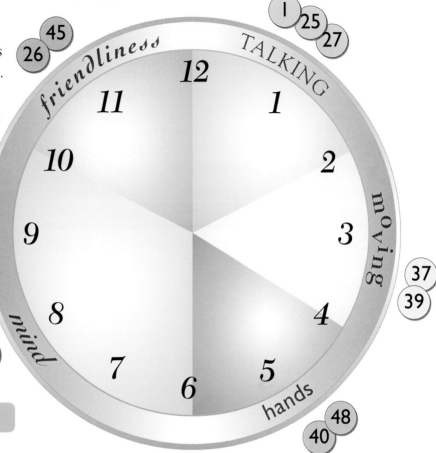

"Keep dancing with **your baby**"

## hands

Increase her awareness of her hands by using all kinds of **tactile stimulation**. Open her hands and tickle her palms. Suitable props: **baby gym, textured bricks**

## moving

Her neck muscles are stronger so concentrate on games which help develop her head control. **Prop her head up** in her baby seat and carry her against your shoulder.

## mind

When she smiles, smile back and **tell her she's clever**. Smiling means she's happy so let her know you're happy too. She loves looking at things so make sure she has plenty of different things to look at — frequently change pictures or **mobiles** hanging over her cot to give lots of interest. Suitable props: **mobile, rattle, frieze**

## TALKING

Now she's making her first vocal sounds your conversation and reaction should be constant. Speak in a **sing-song voice** (most parents do this instinctively) and move around **rocking, swaying** and singing along to music or sing lullabies. Suitable prop: **music tape**

23

# ③ Introducing books

Never underestimate the power of **books as toys**. Your baby's first book (at around one month) should be soft – made of cloth – without words, but include simple **pictures** and bright **colours**, perhaps even textured surfaces. The idea at first is not to read but to enjoy looking and talking together, while you hold her close. Later you can introduce board books and by the time your baby is a year old she should be able to **turn pages by herself**.

## Baby skills

that will benefit from "Introducing books":
• *seeing* • *looking*
• *concentration* • *conceptual thinking* • *memory* • *talking*
• *cognitive thinking*
• *friendliness* • *sharing*
• *manual dexterity*

### *Snuggle up*

With your baby snuggling in the crook of your arm, look at soft cloth books in bright colours. Turn over the pages and talk about the pictures.

### *Look and touch*

Demonstrate textures and flaps in a cloth or board book. Encourage your baby to feel the textures and lift the flaps when she's old enough to join in.

### *Animal sounds*

Show your baby a book of animals. Describe and demonstrate the animals and the noises they make.

### *What do they do?*

Show your older baby a book with pictures of everyday things. Point out things: "There's a car. Cars go VROOM. We go in our car to the supermarket." "There's a kite. Kites fly in the wind. Birds fly too."

# ④ Laughing games

These games teach your baby about the **enjoyment** and **interaction** of play and can also be a **vehicle for learning** quite difficult concepts. You only have to show her fast **tickling** and slow tickling a few times – described and demonstrated of course – and she'll come to expect it. And it's wonderful to laugh – your baby enjoys it and so do you, because to stimulate the unaffected chuckles of a baby is one of the most **rewarding** aspects of parenthood.

**Baby skills**
that will benefit
from "Laughing games":
• *friendliness* • *concept of a joke* • *security*
• *feeling* • *laughing*
• *talking*

### Fast and slow tickles

Tickle your baby's tummy gently with your fingers and tell her what you're doing. Then alternate fast and slow tickles, explaining to her exactly what's going on. Repeat a few more times.

### Blowing "raspberries"

Blow "raspberries" on your baby's tummy – she'll love the tickly feeling and the funny noise. Then blow them in the air – as noisily as you like. Get her to copy you.

### Round and round...

Tickle under your baby's arms and on the soles of her feet – first fast and then slow. Play *Round and round the garden*, either on the palm of her hand as usual or round her tummy button.

### Tongue twisters

Hold your baby face to face. Stick your tongue out, then pull it in. Repeat lots of times. Ask her to copy you and then do it together.

# 2 to 3 months

From now on you'll notice a definite acceleration in your baby's development as he

- wants to interact with everyone around him
- gains control over some of his movements and his muscles strengthen
- can focus on anything at any distance.

## When to play

*Making the most of your baby's wakeful moments helps **bonding** as well as his **social skills**. Now he lets you know when he's in a **playful**, responsive mood and will love it when you join in and show him you understand his needs. **Take your lead from him** though, and **don't force** the issue if he seems tired or grumpy.*

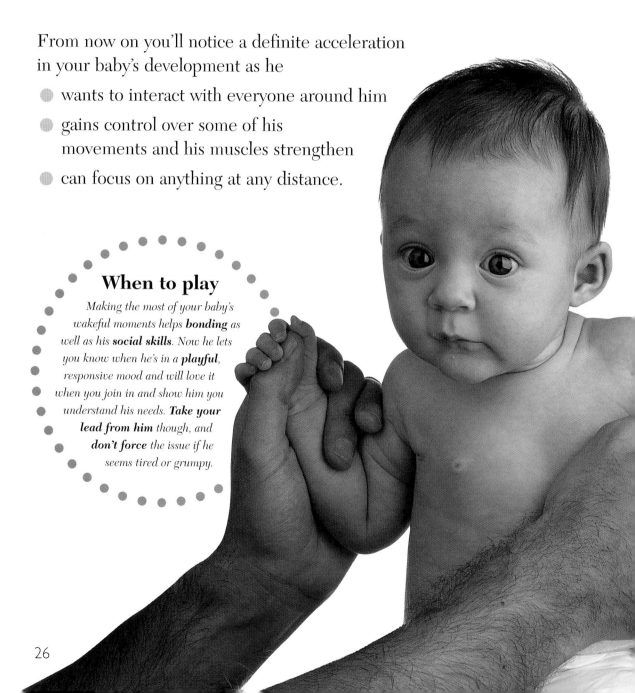

This month you'll see wonderful changes in your baby. He's growing stronger, more vocal and is eager to take a more active part in family life.

# m°vⁱng

Your baby is really learning how to use and control his body now. This means he
• has stronger neck muscles so there's much less head lag when you pull him into a sitting position – his **head is steady** for several minutes when he's held in a sitting position or is propped up, but his back is curved
• can **raise his head** and hold it up when lying on his tummy and he's learned to **lift** his chest off the horizontal by supporting himself a little on his hands, wrists and arms
• practises **bending his knees** while he's lying on his back
• enjoys the control that he now has over his movements and **kicks** and **waves** his arms about when he's lying down – for this reason, never leave him unattended on a changing table or bed.

## TALKING

He's found his voice and takes every opportunity to practise his full range. In doing so he
• makes all kinds of noises to show pleasure – you'll hear **squeals**, **gurgles**, **shouts** and **cooing** sounds
• uses body language too, and will make **excited movements** of his body when he's enjoying himself
• may be starting to add consonants to his vowel sounds, the first normally being **"m"**, then the explosives – you can help him by showing him how to **blow raspberries**
• tends to use "p" and "b" when unhappy and then by three months he'll use more **gutteral** sounds "j" and "k", when **happy**.

"Hear me...
squeal,
gurgle,
shout,
coo"

## *friendliness*

Your baby is learning that being friendly is rewarding because you respond to him with cuddles, love, interest and soothing sounds and to prove this he
• **smiles even more**, knowing that you'll smile back
• will soon **smile spontaneously** in greeting
• turns his head to your voice so that he can see you and welcomes you with a **smile**, **waves** and **kicks**.

## *mind*

Even at this early age he's a keen thinker and he
• is fascinated by his own body and is beginning to understand that he can make it move – the first step in understanding the concept of cause and effect
• enjoys **looking intently** at his hands and fingers while he moves them in front of his face
• is **attracted by moving objects** and has sufficient control over his head to follow a slow-moving object with his eyes. If you hold a brightly coloured toy in front of him, he'll take a moment to focus on it and then his **eyes will follow** it to either side as you move it – in a week or two he'll be able to **focus instantly** and follow the movement easily
• is **very curious about** what goes on around him and watches everything with interest so sit him propped up.

"I welcome my brother with plenty of ...

# smiles, waves and kicks"

## hands

His hand movements are much more purposeful and his **hand-eye co-ordination** is becoming far more accurate. You can see this in the way he
• **pulls** and **plucks** at his clothes with his hands because his **grip** has improved
• **studies** his hands frequently – they provide an ever-present source of interest
• **holds his hand out** as though ready to grasp something he wants, he looks at it intently, but he doesn't reach for it yet – that comes next month
• will **hold a rattle** for a minute or two because he can't loosen his grip voluntarily and when he does drop it he makes no attempt to grasp it again – by three months he'll start to move his hand and discover that he can make sounds with the rattle.

# The Golden Hour

Communication is the key this month – your baby is really beginning to make himself heard and his favourite conversation is with you.

"keep playing music to your baby"

## TALKING

**Respond** to the many different kinds of noises your baby is now beginning to make by talking as much as possible to him while making **full eye contact**. Repeat every sound your baby makes.

## hands

Your baby is very keen on his hands and keeps looking at them so **stimulate** his fingers and palms with finger games. Suitable props: **rattle, bricks with different textures**

## friendliness

Because your baby is beginning to respond to your presence (and conversely, your absence), make a big play of **welcoming him** when you enter the room.

29

# ⑤ Bathtime fun

Bathtime is not only an opportunity for your baby to **enjoy** himself with relative physical **freedom**, it can also be a time for unconscious and **exciting** learning. Water splashes, pours, runs, trickles, fills things, allows objects to float or sink, providing your baby with a laboratory of scientific experimentation.

> **SAFETY FIRST**
> Never leave your baby alone in the bath, even when he can sit unaided, and always use a safety mat to prevent him from slipping.

*Before your baby can sit:*

### Knee bends

With you or your partner supporting your baby's shoulders, head and neck, gently bend his knees in the water to encourage kicking.

### Make a splash

Hold your baby as for the knee bends and gently bend his elbows to encourage him to start splashing. Then massage his body with a soft sponge or flannel.

*When your baby can sit:*

### Diving ducks

Put some plastic ducks in the bath. Quack and see if your baby copies you. Push them under and then watch them pop up again.

### Fill and pour

Show your baby how to fill and empty a plastic cup. Give him other containers to fill and empty out.

### Baby skills

that will benefit from "Bathtime fun":
• *having fun* • *overcoming fear*
• *mobility* • *cause and effect*
• *head control* • *sitting*
• *understanding concepts*
• *imagination*

**2** to **12** months  mind ● talking ✓ moving ✓ hands ✓ friendliness

# ⑥ Hubble bubble

Soap bubbles provide hours of **delight** and **fascination** for babies from the age of about three months and they continue to be a **source of fun** right through childhood. Start with safe baby bubbles in the bath and progress to blowing bubbles through a traditional plastic ring so that your baby can try to **catch** them.

### Baby skills

that will benefit from "Hubble bubble":
- *talking* • *conversation*
- *breath control* • *friendliness*
- *experimentation* • *seeing*
- *anticipation*

## Foamy fun

Fill the bath with frothy bubbles. Lift up a handful of bubbly foam and blow it gently onto your baby's tummy. Encourage your baby to pat the bubbles and watch them float about.

## Soapy hands

Make your hands really wet and soapy and then collect a smooth layer of soap bubble inside the ring made by closing your forefinger onto the tip of your thumb. Tell your baby to watch very carefully and then very slowly, blow into the film of soap – see how big you can make the bubble before it bursts. The bigger the better – your baby will love it!

## Catching bubbles

Buy a bubble dispenser and blow lots of bubbles close to your baby. As his ability to reach and grasp grows he'll have endless fun trying to catch the bubbles as they float into view and watching them pop by themselves. As he learns to point (at around eight or nine months) encourage him to pop the bubbles himself with his finger. Make sure you use bubble mixture that won't sting his eyes in case a bubble pops in his face.

---

*3* to *12* months ✓ mind ✓ talking ○ moving ● hands ✓ friendliness

# 3 to 4 months

You'll notice a big change in the way your baby relates to the world around her during this month. This is because she

- is more wakeful during the day
- is less likely to be fretful and colicky in the evening
- recognizes familiar faces and places
- loves a joke and is ready to show she's learned how to laugh.

## Fingers and toes

*At this age your baby can make her **hands** and **feet** do some of the things she wants. She thinks **fingers** and **toes** have the same importance because she hasn't yet learned that hands can do more than feet. That's why it's important to play **games** with her toes as well as games with her fingers.*

Your baby's obvious fascination with her hands and feet is delightful. But this is more than just a way of passing time – she's learning some valuable lessons.

## m⁰vⁱng

Your baby wants to be propped up or held in a sitting position so that she can look around and take part in what's going on. It should be easier for her to do this now she can
• sit with a **straight back**, not with the curved back of the previous couple of months
• **partially control her head movements**, although she'll need a bit of support as her head still wobbles a bit as she turns it
• completely **raise her chest** off the mat when lying on her tummy, supporting herself on her widely separated arms – she tries to look straight ahead in this position, although she can't quite manage it yet.

## TALKING

Your baby will start trying to hold a "conversation" with you now that she
• makes more than simple vowel and consonant sounds
• tries to **imitate** sentences like yours by stringing sounds together or coming out with "words" like "gaga" or "ahgoo"
• uses quite a **repertoire** of sounds and by 16 weeks she'll **express her feelings**, many of which signify delight, by chuckling, laughing and squealing
• can **blow** through her lips – she shows off her new skill by blowing bubbles.

## hands

Her hands and fingers are becoming her favourite plaything – they're always available – and she
• spends ages **studying** her fingers moving
• can **move** her hands and feet together and apart **on purpose**
• can **hold a toy** when she keeps her hands together – it's a marvellous discovery
• can **put one foot on the opposite knee** and can roll her feet so that the soles are flat on the mat – essential for learning to walk in later months
• **shakes a rattle** to hear the noise, although she can't pick it up by herself yet
• can stretch her hands out to **reach for a toy**, but she misjudges the distance and overshoots.

## She loves to laugh

*Your baby will learn how to be **funny**, make **jokes** and enjoy herself through any game that makes her laugh or elicits laughter from you. All babies love to make someone laugh – it's instant feedback. She'll know you're pleased with her and she knows she's got your attention – her favourite pastime! **Laughter** is good for you both as it **boosts** the immune system.*

## "keep up a running commentary

with your baby"

## friendliness

She's naturally **out-going** and at this stage not at all shy. This is clearly seen in the way she

• **looks**, **smiles**, **grunts** and **coos** at anyone who speaks to her or pays her attention
• knows you and the rest of the family and **recognizes** family **pets**
• **gets lonely** and lets you know she doesn't like being alone for too long when she's awake
• **stops crying** when you go to her, showing pleasure at your presence
• **jigs** her body when she sees you
• **uses laughter** to charm you.

## mind

Your baby's visual perception is maturing and she

• can assess the different shapes and sizes of things and their position relative to one another (see Activity 9) because she's **curious about detail** and notices the edges of objects
• **loves patterns** of different kinds and can distinguish colours
• can **recognize a photograph** of a loved one, especially you!

Her brain is growing at a tremendous rate, which can be seen in her increased curiosity. In particular she

• **takes an interest in everything** when propped up into a sitting position
• shows interest in anything new: faces, toys, sounds and situations
• has the **confidence** to look around with interest when taken into a strange room
• recognizes and **shows pleasure** in daily rituals, such as bathtime and feeding
• **enjoys jokes** like "beeping" her nose.

# The Golden Hour

Your baby's becoming really good with her hands. She's beginning to **hold** things if you put them in her hand and **swipe** at them if they're dangling within her reach. She's also making great **intellectual strides**.

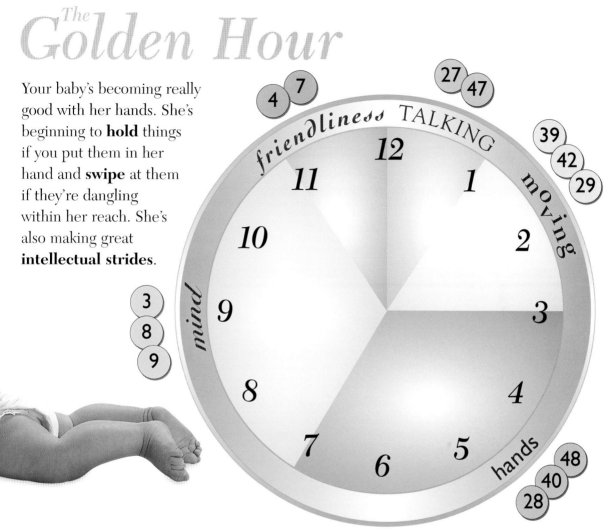

## mind

Her eyes and brain are able to do so much, including **distinguishing** the size, shape and relative position of things. Try the Baby Brain Teaser (Activity 9) at 16 weeks to check this. She **anticipates rituals** like feeds and baths so be theatrical about them and always **describe** what you're doing.

Suitable props: **mirror, mobile**

## "Tickle me to …
# see me chuckle"

### hands

Keep giving her a **rattle** to shake so she can make a noise herself. Give her **toys** to hold between both hands and set up a **baby gym** where she can reach it.

Suitable props: **rattle, baby gym**

### moving

She wants to sit up so **prop her up** as much as possible. Encourage further head control with **baby press-ups** by lying her on her tummy so that she'll raise her body and head off the mat with her arms.

# ⑦ Hands and fingers

The most enjoyable baby games are nearly always packed with **unconscious learning**. Every game has a **teachable moment** as long as you use a light touch and are aware of when your baby has had enough. Hand and finger games are no exception because from about three months your baby knows **how to use her hands and fingers**. These games and those in Activity 29 for feet and toes are interchangeable.

## Baby skills

that will benefit from "Hands and fingers":
• *fine finger movement* • *manual dexterity* • *co-ordination*
• *friendliness* • *humour*
• *feelings and emotions*
• *imitation* • *talking*

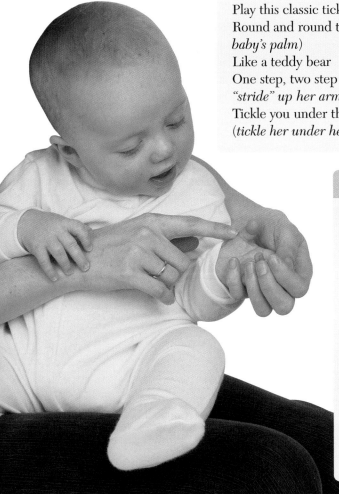

### Round and round the garden

Play this classic tickle game:
Round and round the garden (*circle your finger round your baby's palm*)
Like a teddy bear
One step, two step (*make your forefinger and middle finger "stride" up her arm*)
Tickle you under there
(*tickle her under her armpit or chin*).

### Tommy Thumb

Play this to identify your baby's separate fingers:
Tommy Thumb, Tommy Thumb, where are you?
Here I am, here I am, how do you do?
(*Wiggle your baby's thumb or your own*)
Do the same with the other fingers, naming them as follows:
Peter Pointer (*index finger*); Toby Tall (*middle finger*); Ruby Ring (*ring finger*); Baby Small (*little finger*)
End with
Fingers all, fingers all, where are you?
Here we are, here we are, how do you do?
(*wiggle and shake all five fingers*).

# ⑧ Peep-bo

Peep-bo (or "Peepo" or "Peekaboo") is one of the best-known baby games. It's so familiar it's hard to remember that there are two important concepts hidden in this game. The first is that even when your baby can't see something it nonetheless **exists**. This feeds her natural **curiosity** to find out about the world around her. The second is learning to **anticipate** what comes next and **waiting** for it to happen. This helps **memory**, the acceptance of routine and the difficult concept of **"the future"** – what will happen next.

### Hide…

Simply put your hands over your face: "Where's Daddy gone?" Then take them away again dramatically: "PEEP-BO!"

### …and seek

Hold a blanket in front of your baby's face: "Where's Mummy gone?" Drop the blanket: "Peep-bo!" Do it again, but encourage her to grab the blanket herself: "Peep-bo! You've found Mummy!"

### Where's Teddy?

By eight or nine months she'll hide herself under a blanket or towel so you can take turns with Peep-bo. You can also play Peep-bo with a teddy or soft toy. As well as "Where has Teddy gone?", ask "WHEN will Teddy come back?" to reinforce a concept of future events.

### Baby skills

that will benefit from "Peep-bo":
• *looking* • *observation*
• *concentration* • *memory*
• *anticipation* • *trust*
• *concept of absence*

# 4 to 5 months

Your baby is becoming aware of new and strange situations and is learning how to express his feelings. Now's the time to introduce him to a sense of achievement with more games and toys. During the fifth month he

- wants to learn and imitate
- starts to concentrate hard
- begins to control his hands
- loves to join in games.

## Gaze aversion

*Your baby can't say no yet, but if you're tuned in to him while you play you can soon tell when he's had enough. He'll **avert his gaze** and **refuse** to make eye contact. This is the time to cuddle him or **distract** him with something. If you don't respond to this gaze aversion your baby can only resort to **crying** to tell you how he feels.*

## hands

Your baby is beginning to realize that his hands are great **tools** and he

- has found his **toes** and discovered he can pull them into his **mouth**
- **puts everything**, including his fists, into his **mouth** as it's his most sensitive area
- tries to **grasp** his toys for the first time with his hand wide open, palm down and mainly by **curling his little finger** in to his palm – he can only do this with quite large objects because he hasn't any fine finger movements yet
- **reaches out** for everything, grabbing and hitting, but beware – he loves long hair!
- loves **crumpling** paper, clothes or blankets.

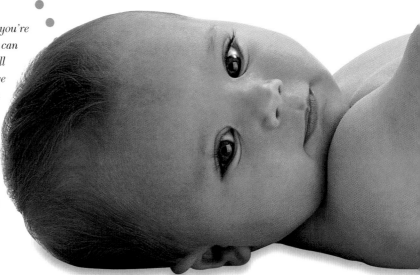

# By now his personality shines through. He's no longer the little stranger he once was – you know his needs and he's confident you'll meet them.

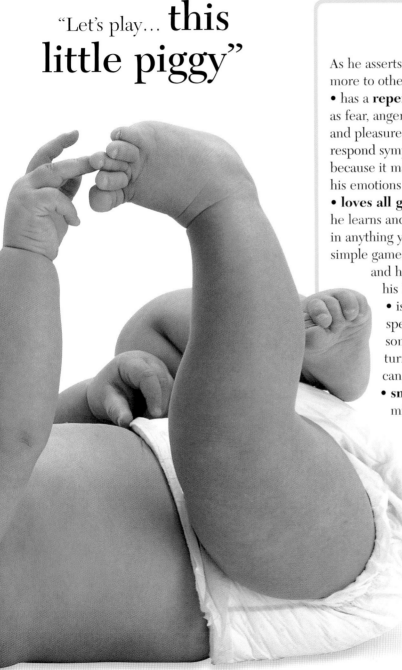

"Let's play... **this little piggy"**

## *mind*

As he asserts his personality and relates more to other people your baby

- has a **repertoire of emotions** such as fear, anger, disgust, frustration, sadness and pleasure to which he wants you to respond sympathetically – and you should because it makes him feel comfortable with his emotions

- **loves all games** because this is the way he learns and as he wants to learn he'll join in anything you suggest – he'll even make up simple games like splashing the bath water and he studies intently the effect of his hands and feet in the water

- is learning to **concentrate**, and spends a long time just looking at something he holds in his hands, turning it over for as long as he can, although he often drops it

- **smiles at his reflection** in a mirror, although he doesn't yet realize it's actually himself

- moves his arms and legs to **attract your attention** and makes noises to **call you** to him

- **loves the breast or bottle** and shows this by patting it when feeding.

# m⁰ᵥⁱng

His muscles are developing fast. He's gaining all-important head control so he can
• **move his head from side to side** easily, without it wobbling
• **keep his head in line** with his body when he's pulled to sitting without it lagging behind – **a major developmental milestone**
• **keep his head steady** when sitting up, even if you gently rock him to and fro
• **raise his chest** off the floor when lying on his tummy and **look forward steadily**, supporting himself on his arms.

## TALKING

During this month your baby tries out different vowels and consonants. He's also developing many non-verbal signals to communicate his needs. For example, he
• **clings** to you dramatically when he doesn't want to be put down
• may **push you away** when he's unhappy and doesn't want your attention
• **turns his head** away if he dislikes something.

### Tone of voice

*Because your baby is **disturbed by an angry tone of voice** he'll stop when you sound displeased to see if you really disapprove of him. This response is the basis of all future discipline – all that's needed is a change in the tone of your voice. He **loves a friendly voice** and will do almost anything to hear one, even refraining from doing what he wants.*

## *friendliness*

Your baby is learning how to express his feelings in a variety of ways. By the end of this month he
• **knows your voice** and its modulations very well and doesn't like the different tone of voice you use when you say **"No"**, although he doesn't yet know what it means
• eagerly **smiles** to greet people he knows
• uses body movements, facial expressions and sounds as well as crying, to **show his moods**.

# The Golden Hour

It's only going to be another month or so before your baby can **sit up unaided**. This skill is a **vital step** towards learning to walk so help him to strengthen his neck and back muscles in preparation.

## "keep smiling

at your baby"

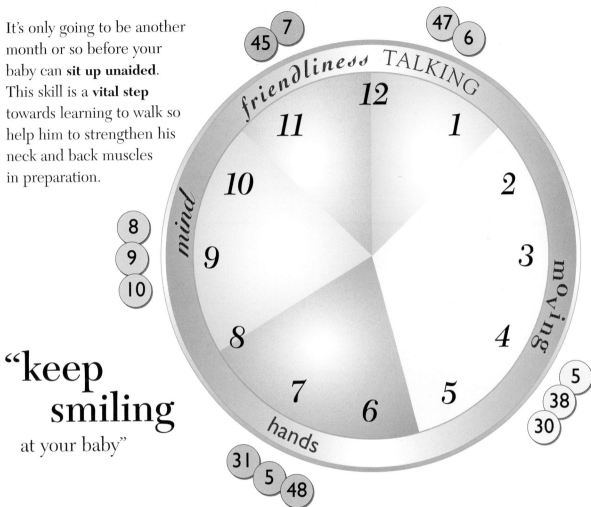

## m o v i n g

Now that his upper body is strong and mobile and head control is complete, you can play **bouncing games** on your knee. He may also start to **roll** from his front to his back so play floor games and roly-poly.

## hands

He's **grasping toys** with an open palm so always put them within his reach. He loves his toes too, so continue to play **foot and toe games**.
Suitable props: **ball, rattle, textured bricks**

## mind

He's desperate to **learn** and to **imitate** so try new games with **rhymes** and **actions**. Give him interesting objects to hold and examine to combine **manipulation** and **intellectual** skills.
Suitable props: **mobile, rattle**

## ⑨ Baby brain teaser

When your baby is just 16 weeks old see how intelligent he is by playing this game. It's staggering, but already he's ace at non-verbal **reasoning** and can make some **distinctions** in the size of shapes, like **big** and **small.**

### Making shape cards

Take four pieces of card at least 21 cm (8½ in) deep. On the first, draw a small circle above a large circle; on the second, a small diamond above a large diamond; on the third, a small triangle above a large triangle; and finally, a large triangle above a small triangle (see below). Colour in the shapes using a bright, solid colour such as red or blue.

**Baby skills**

*that will benefit from "Baby brain teaser":*
- *perception* • *observation*
- *spatial awareness*
- *concentration*
- *seeing*

### Circles and diamonds

Show your baby the circle card followed by the diamond card. Your baby will be able to perceive the relationship between the small shape above the large shape.

### Triangles

Now show your baby the third card (a small triangle on top of a large triangle). If your baby has grasped the idea of small over big from the previous two cards he won't show any interest at all in this picture. If, however, you then show him the fourth card on which there's a large triangle above a small triangle – a different concept altogether – you'll probably find that he shows renewed interest.

# ⑩ Yes and no

From four months your baby will **"stop"** when you say "No" in a firm voice because it implies temporary withdrawal of your approval – the **first step towards discipline.** These games help him understand that "No" has another use that is much more straightforward – **it's the opposite of "Yes"** and introduces him to the general concepts of **negative** and **positive** – the basis of all **intellectual analysis.** These simple games use the non-verbal signals of **head shaking** and **nodding** that precede speech.

**Baby skills**

that will benefit from "Yes and no": • *cognitive thinking* • *remembering words* • *observation* • *conversation* • *taking turns* • *body language* • *using a word (non-verbally with meaning)*

## *Questions and answers*

Sit with your baby on the floor with some toys in front of you. Choose a toy or brick and show your baby that you're picking it up. Very deliberately hide it behind your back. Then ask him, ^ "Has Daddy got the brick?" Encourage him to nod his head while you nod yours and say, "Yes!" Do it again until he gets the idea. Then hide the brick under a blanket or mat. Say, "Can Sam and Daddy see the brick?" and shake your head, "No!"

## *"Is this a...?"*

Using a simple picture book of familiar animals ask your baby if he knows what the different animals are. Point to the cat and ask him, "Is this a cat? Yes!" Nod your head vigorously and encourage him to as well. Then point to the duck. "Is this a cat? No!" Shake your head and get him to copy you. After a few turns he'll be doing it without your help. Praise him every time he gets it right.

**4** to **12** months  ✓ mind  ✓ talking  ● moving  ● hands  ● friendliness

# 5 to 6 months

The sixth month is a watershed for your baby because she

- begins to understand that people or things still exist even though she can't see them
- starts following the pattern of conversation with her wide range of vocal sounds
- may even be sitting up unaided for short periods by the end of the month
- is beginning to use both hands to co-ordinate the holding and guiding of objects, such as her bottle.

Your baby is increasingly mobile - she can't wait to be on th

She's starting to babble and wants to make herself heard. Her hand-eye co-ordination is getting better so she's rather pleased with herself – quite right too!

## move!

Her increasing **strength** and **mobility** means that she
- is accomplished at **press-ups** – she's able to support her head, chest and abdomen off the floor on her hands alone when they're fairly close together and in this position she can **hold her head up** and **look forward**; she also tries to **take her weight on one hand**
- can sit up unaided

# moving

for a few seconds supporting herself with her hands between her legs
- **can sit supported** by cushions in her highchair for a few minutes
- lifts her head in preparation when you show her you're going to pull her up to sit
- can **roll right over** from her tummy on to her back
- wants to take all her weight when you stand her up on your lap, although her knees will sag – she **flexes** and **extends** her legs by **bouncing up and down**.

## TALKING

She's getting the hang of **taking turns** in conversation and **trying new sounds**. Listen as she
- attempts to converse with her **mirror image** and has a "conversation" of gurgles with herself
- is intent on **imitating** your conversation and **uses her tongue** a lot, poking it out and playing with it between her lips
- has a growing **repertoire** of speech sounds, especially the **blowing** and **raspberry** sounds that she practises often

- begins to respond to her **name** – use her name at every opportunity so she'll start to achieve a **sense of self** and feel important
- makes special sounds to **attract your attention**, even trying a **cough**
- starts to join real vowels and real consonants together in a simple way, saying **"ka"**, **"da"**, **"ma"** and **"ergh"**
- **understands** bits of what you say, such as, "Here's your bottle", "Daddy's coming," "Yes" and "No"
- begins to **babble** – repeats sounds over and over, listens, then tries them out again.

# hands

By now she has much greater control over her hands and she
• is able to **grasp** a cube with her whole hand, still leading with her little finger
• can consciously **let go** of something and will **drop** one object to take another
• can **hold her bottle** between two hands and can **direct it** to her mouth without help
• still **grasps her feet** when lying on her back and puts her toes in her mouth (a boy may grasp his penis)
• **looks closely** at objects that she's holding when propped up and turns them over
• is longing to **feed herself** and will do so if you give her safe finger foods that are easy to grasp.

# *mind*

Your baby knows her own mind and can make herself understood. She also
• continues to enjoy looking at herself in the **mirror**, but her fascination has gone a step further – she now **vocalizes to the reflection** as if it's another baby
• can **anticipate** someone appearing when she hears footsteps approaching, she **gets excited** because she knows someone is there even though she can't actually see them
• knows fear and **becomes anxious** when you leave the room and she can't see you any more
• uses many different **gestures** to make her wants known, especially showing her **likes** and **dislikes**
• is **curious** about where her rattle has gone when she **drops** it and **looks** for it
• **loves games** like "Peep-bo" and will laugh if you hide her head with a napkin
• is better able to **grab** things as she's beginning to judge the distance between herself and the object she wants (**"hand-eye co-ordination"**).

# *friendliness*

She's **showing love** for the first time. You'll notice that she
• makes lots of advances to you and **wants to touch** you but because she hasn't developed refined movement, she tends to pat you roughly
• **loves your face** – she'll nuzzle and stroke it and she may also grab a handful of hair!
• may begin to be **shy with strangers** towards the end of this month – she'll **bury her head** on your chest if someone she doesn't know speaks to her or you, and may cry if a stranger picks her up.

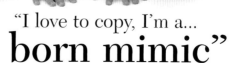

"I love to copy, I'm a...
# born mimic"

# The Golden Hour

Your baby is becoming increasingly **demonstrative** and **wants to show her love** for you through touch and vocalization. Act out being loving with sounds like "ah" and gestures and strokes.

## "keep singing

to your baby"

*friendliness*

mind

hands

TALKING

moving

29
8
4

27
6
44

3
33

12
11
28

30
41
42

12
11
10
9
8
7
6
5
4
3
2
1

## *friendliness*

Get her to **touch your face** and say "Hello" as she does so. Put a mirror in a position where she can see herself and help her to **pat her image**. There are many games you can play with reflections. Teach her to **show love** with lots of patting and stroking of pets and cuddly toys and show her books with pictures of mother animals and their babies.
Suitable props: **books, cuddly toys**

## TALKING

**Talk to her as much as you can** – tell her what you're doing all the time, point out interesting things, especially **animals**, when you're out and about. **Repeat** phrases and praise her when she appears to understand you. **Sing songs** and say **rhymes** to her. Play **clapping** games together. **Read** books together, pointing, naming and making the sounds of animals.
Suitable props: **music tape, animal book**

# ⑪ Clapping games

Games involving **rhythm, rhyming,** accentuation and **music** all foster **speech** on their own – together they're formidable. Clapping games are fun because they're rhythmic, noisy and musical. Hand **clapping** and **patting** are skills that develop fairly early so she can quickly **join in** and be on equal terms with you.

**Baby skills**

that will benefit from "Clapping games":
• hand control • hand-eye co-ordination • bi-manual co-ordination • concentration • memory • observation • speech • imitation • participation

## Here's a ball for baby

You and your baby can act this out together:
Here's a ball for baby
Big and fat and round
(*cup your hands in a ball*)
Here's a baby's hammer
See how it can pound
(*hammer with your fist*)
Here are baby's soldiers
Standing in a row
(*point fingers upwards*)
Here is baby's music
Clapping, clapping so
(*clap your hands in time while humming a well-known tune*).

## Pat-a-cake

Clap your baby's hand against your own until she's able to clap.
Pat-a-cake, pat-a-cake, baker's man (*clap hands in rhythm*)
Bake me a cake as fast as you can ("*stir*" *the cake mix*)
Pat it (*pat your baby's hand*) and prick it (*poke your baby's hand with a finger*) and mark it with B (*trace a "B" on your baby's palm*)
And put it in the oven for Baby and me (*mime sliding the cake into the oven*).

**5** to **12** months ✓mind ✓talking ○ moving ✓hands ✓friendliness

## ⑫ Bricks and blocks

Traditional wooden bricks and blocks are stimulating in all sorts of ways. Long before your baby can **stack** them she can **clasp** one, which she'll **study** carefully and turn over in her hands. Then she'll be able to **hold one** in each hand and will soon learn to **bang** them together to make a satisfyingly loud noise. She'll try stacking from the age of about 11 months when she's mastered the skill of **letting go** accurately as well as **holding**.

### Baby skills

that will benefit from "Bricks and blocks":
• *refining grasp* • *letting go*
• *manipulation* • *hand-eye co-ordination* • *concentration*
• *cause and effect* •
*strength* • *placing*

### Pick a brick

Put different-shaped bricks into her hand. Describe their differences: "This round brick is red. It rolls along the floor." "This yellow brick is square; it's got straight edges. You can put another brick on top of it." Let her examine them and choose which one she wants to pick up.

### All fall down

When she can sit up, build a tower of bricks in front of her. See how quickly she can knock them down. Bang two bricks together, one in each hand, or get her to bang a row of bricks on the floor using the brick she's holding.

### Building blocks

Once she's got the hang of letting go, carefully encourage her to build her own tower – first one brick on top of another, then more. Build a bridge of bricks and show her how to push a toy car or roll a brick underneath.

# 6 to 7 months

Now your baby will be sitting up unaided and this increases his independence and confidence enormously. So he

- is becoming a lot more assertive
- practises his rapidly developing vocal skills
- is growing more sociable.

## Baby talk

*Reinforce your baby's delight in vocalization by repeating the recognizable sounds he makes, like "ba", "da" and "ka". If he **babbles a lot** try to copy his voice variations and then make a new sound and wait for him to answer. He'll soon learn to **take turns** and may **try to copy** the sounds you make.*

No wonder your baby seems more outgoing and settled now. Being able to sit up by himself gives him an exciting new view of the world around him.

## *mind*

Your baby is really beginning to understand his surroundings now and his memory is improving – he can **anticipate daily routines** and the ritual of familiar games. See this in the way he

• **loves his reflection** in a mirror so much that he starts patting it – he'll pat and stroke your face too in a show of profound affection and he's getting used to feeling love and expressing it

• **knows his name** and will respond to it

• **copies you** – if you put out your tongue he'll put out his

• **anticipates** the actions of a game you repeat over and over

• can **find an object partly hidden** under a cloth and loves playing "Peep-bo"

• is very close to **understanding** the meaning of "No!" – he responds by restraining himself, drawing back and looking at you questioningly for more information. You should then repeat "No!".

## TALKING

Your baby is really beginning to experiment with conversations to himself as well as with you so he

• **babbles** to no-one in particular because he loves the sound of his own voice

• **initiates conversations** instead of waiting for you to start

• makes many recognizable sounds

• tries to **imitate sounds** you make, in particular animal sounds – "quack, quack"

• has an orchestra of high- and low-pitched sounds that have their own non-verbal meaning

• makes a **nasal sound** for the first time

• can make **chewing movements** with his gums and so can eat solids – chewing makes him aware of his mouth and helps speech development.

## *friendliness*

He likes company but he's more self-contained and happy with his own company too. He

• **recognizes** other babies as being like himself and reaches out to them in friendship

• **pats** other babies or his own reflection, just as he pats you

• **vocalizes** to himself and other babies, just as he does to you

• **joins in** games like "Pat-a-cake" and "This little piggy"

• is very **sociable** and wants you to understand him so he laughs, coughs, cries, squeals, blows bubbles, smiles and frowns to converse with you.

# m o v i n g

He'll make great strides this month. Now he

- can lift one hand off the floor in the **press-up** position and take all his weight on one arm
- can **sit quite safely** without support
- is strong enough to **lift his head** to look around when he's lying on his back
- can **roll over** from his back to his tummy (much harder than the other way round)
- can use his muscles to **straighten his legs** without wobbling so that he can take his whole weight steadily when you stand him on your lap
- **bounces** by bending and stretching his ankles, knees and hips.

# hands

Your baby's grasp is becoming more refined and he

- **reaches** for a cube with his fingers instead of palming it with an open hand
- can easily **pass a toy** from one hand to another
- reaches for a toy with one hand and not two as previously
- **holds** on to one cube in one hand and takes another cube offered to him in the other.

His co-ordination is also improving, he

- **bangs** with the flat of his hand
- feeds himself with finger foods and can **hold a spoon**, although he's not very accurate with it yet
- is able to drink from a two-handled cup.

## Object permanence

*Your baby will begin to work out that an object still exists, even though he can't see it, whether it's his mother or a toy – psychologists call this "person permanence" or "object permanence". With help he'll be able to find an object under a cloth if there's a little bit visible. A month or two later he'll learn to look for it even though he can't see it.*

# The Golden Hour

His grasp is becoming more and more precise – it's the key to so much future learning and independence. He's also putting things expertly into his mouth to explore so don't let him hold very small objects that he can swallow. He has so much more control over his hands and arms now.

*friendliness* TALKING *moving* *hands* *mind*

29 44 27 47 14 13 3 5 38 45 23 12 11

12 11 1 10 2 9 3 8 4 7 6 5

## hands

Give him finger foods and his bottle to hold and introduce a two-handled cup. Give him small objects to hold between his fingers (but not so small he can swallow and choke on them). He loves to **make a noise** so show him how to bang with the flat of his hand and play **"Pat-a-cake"**. Suitable props: **ball, bricks, rattle**

## moving

Now he can roll over from his back to his tummy try some floor games. Don't be afraid to be a bit silly – he's developing a **great sense of humour** and it's good for you too. On his tummy he can rest on one hand so give him things to reach when in this position to improve his balance and strength.

## mind

His mind and his speech are in full flow, he loves hand and **clapping games** and he'll try to **imitate animal sounds** if you make them. Always show him a picture or the real thing as well so he can learn all the attributes of an animal – what it looks like, sounds like and what it can do. He **loves books** of all kinds.

53

# ⑬ Hide and come back

This game is a direct follow-on to "Peep-bo", which helps your baby to understand that **things still exist even if she can't see them**. This is a step further on the Skill Map since it encourages her to find out **WHERE things go when she can't see them**. This knowledge helps her to feel secure when familiar things go because she knows they come back again – and this can include her parents.

**Baby skills**

that will benefit
from "Hide and come back":
• *curiosity* • *cognitive thinking*
• *concentration* • *achievement*
• *understanding* • *concepts of gone and return* • *concepts of hidden and found* • *rhythm*
• *language* • *balance*
• *head control*

## Where's it gone?

Sit with your baby on the floor. Hold a squeaky toy or teddy where she can't quite reach it and make it squeak. Then hide it behind your back. If she tries to look for it, give it to her with lots of praise. If she's still unsure, squeak it again so she has an aural clue.

## Two little dickie birds

Sing this with actions:
Two little dickie birds sitting on a wall
   (*hold up your forefingers*)
One named Peter, the other named Paul
   (*wiggle your fingers*)
Fly away Peter
   (*hide one hand behind your back*)
Fly away Paul
   (*hide the other hand behind your back*)
Come back Peter
   (*show your hand again*)
Come back Paul
   (*show your other hand*).

**6** to **12** months ✓mind ✓talking ✓moving ✓hands ✓friendliness

# ⑭ More about books

Books are some of the best toys because they're interesting and you're nearly always involved in looking at them with your baby, which she'll love. Books with **storylines** encourage your baby to find out **what happens next** so they stimulate her **imagination, memory** and **intellect.** Coincidentally they promote many other emerging skills – even physical ones like **pointing.** Have books on hand all the time – bedtime, bathtime, car journeys or naps. Leave soft ones in her cot at night.

**Baby skills**

that will benefit from "More about books":
• *concentration* • *remembering a sequence of events* • *turning over pages* • *recognizing pictures and things* • *knowing the meaning of words* • *naming* • *saying words with meaning*

## Storytime

Read very simple stories with few words and big, simple pictures. Books with animal pictures are ideal, especially if they have mother and baby combinations. Just point out the picture, name the animal (cat) and its baby (kitten), demonstrate the sound it makes and make up a story about each. Point all the time. Babies also love pictures of other babies.

## Turn the page

Whatever you read, describe and demonstrate how to turn pages. Your baby needs fine finger movements to turn over only one page (from 11 to 12 months) but will try to turn over pages much earlier in her eagerness to get on.

## Family stories

Your older baby will love hearing her own name and those of her family in stories. When looking at picture books, make up the stories to include your baby and Mummy, Daddy, Grandma and the pet dog as characters. It will enhance her self-image and her own idea of family.

# 7 to 8 months

Now your baby is beginning to understand that she's a separate person – and the people close to her are special. During this month she

- may start being shy and seem afraid of strangers
- will show that she's developed a very special attachment to you.

## "Just look at me now!"

### *friendliness*

Your baby may become wary of people she doesn't know well, but this is a way of showing her affection and preference for the people she knows best and who care for her. See how she
- responds if you say, "kiss" to her – she'll **move her body** towards you and make kissing noises
- will **pat or stroke** a furry toy or pet to show affection
- **loves older children** and tries to touch them, but from the safety of your arms
- **starts crying** when you leave her and stops when you return or pick her up, showing that you love her.

### TALKING

She's quite capable of making her feelings and needs known to you by her facial expressions and the noises she makes. Although real speech is still a few months off she
- is starting to **combine syllables** (this may develop slightly later in boys than girls) so **"da"** becomes **"dada"**, **"ma"** becomes **"mama"**, **"guh"** becomes **"guhguh"** and so on
- tries to **make animal noises** quite readily now if she sees a picture of an animal or a cat or a dog in the street.

Your baby is learning to express love – she leaves you in no doubt that she loves you and is never happier than when you show you love her too.

# mind

You'll notice increasing signs that your baby understands what you say, even though she can't speak words with meaning. Around this time she

- can **remember opposites** through touch (hot/cold; hard/soft)
- **understands some differences** (Mummy's coat/Baby's coat)
- can begin to **judge the size** of objects up to a metre away
- **understands phrases** if they're part of routines so when you go into the bathroom she understands, "It's time for a bath"
- understands that "No!" means stop, don't do it or don't touch
- **shows determination** and reaches for a toy she really wants – she's persistent and may cry with frustration if she's unsuccessful
- **plays** with her toys, examining and concentrating on them at length
- is **becoming very assertive** about showing she wants to feed herself.

## Don't impose a timetable

*It's exciting when your baby really starts to take an interest in her toys and her surroundings and seems to be on the brink of crawling. But remember that you can't impose a timetable on her. What you can do though, is* **be there as a willing playmate to encourage** *her – she'll start to crawl only when she's ready. Try not to compare her with other babies of the same age –* **all babies are different**.

# m⁰ᵥⁱng

Your baby's **independence** and **determination** will inevitably lead to propulsion of some kind if only to get hold of things beyond her reach. So she
• will try to move her body to a toy that's out of reach – to do this she'll probably work out that she can **rock her body** backwards and forwards to get up enough momentum to reach the toy
• learns an important lesson from this **"launching off"** action – that her whole body can reach something her hands cannot on their own
• loves standing on your knee – her legs are strong now and **support her weight** easily with her knees and hips.

## hands

Her ability to keep herself amused for quite long periods on her own is helped by her increasing manual dexterity. You'll find she
• **bangs her hands** – and toys – on any surface
• has a sufficiently **fine grasp** to pull paper apart and tear it
• **reaches** for a toy and picks it up with her fingers not her palm, but for now she's still using *all* her fingers and thumb
• **points** at things with her index finger – the sign that her mature **pincer grip** is about to emerge.

### Shuffling up

*Encourage your baby to shuffle on her bottom as it gives her the thrill of being mobile and an idea of how much* **fun** *she can have once she's* **on the move***. Sit on the floor just beyond her reach and* **stretch out your arms***, calling her name. Catch her if she topples and* **praise her** *when she succeeds.*

"Hands are for…

# gripping, pointing, banging"

# The Golden Hour

Your baby's personality is really emerging – she knows who her favourite people are. She really dislikes your absence and shows fear and anxiety when you leave her. She's wary of strangers so introduce her to new people gradually.

# "keep repeating rhymes"

## *friendliness*

She's **very affectionate** towards you and people she knows. She loves to **kiss** and **pat** you. Reciprocate with lots of cuddles, kisses and continue the baby massage. She's interested in other children too, and will reach out to them. Now's the time to introduce **playmates.**
Suitable props: **cuddly toys**

## *mind*

Now that she **understands "Yes"** and **"No"**, use them all the time. Be extra positive about "Yes" and be careful about saying "No". Try not to make "No" an automatic reaction because she'll soon figure out you're just pulling rank. **Always make "Yes!" a celebration.**

## TALKING

Now that she has got as far as two-syllable sounds, recite **nursery rhymes** which have lots of **repetition** and remember to carry on **repeating back to her** any "words" she says. Read, **point** and name with books all the time.
Suitable props: **books**

# ⑮ Roly poly

For the first few months all physical movement contributes to your baby's Skill Map for walking. **Head control** is on that map early on and without it your baby would never walk. Similarly it's just as important for him to **strengthen his trunk** so that he can **twist** and **turn** his body **in preparation for crawling**. Rolling from his back to his tummy precedes rolling from his tummy to his back, which is harder and comes a few weeks later.

**Baby skills**

that will benefit from "Roly poly":
- *rolling* • *mobility*
- *strength* • *co-ordination*
- *adventurousness*
- *curiosity*

## Roll to daddy

Lie down on the floor beside your baby. Call his name and get him to roll over towards you. Give him a big kiss. Now do it from the other side. Clever boy!

## Roll over

Lie him on the floor facing away from you. Call his name and encourage him to roll over towards you. Repeat on the other side. Praise him when he succeeds.

## Find the toy

Lie him down with his back to a favourite toy. Call his name and encourage him to roll over and get the toy. Give it to him when he succeeds.

## Family fun

When he can roll over easily show him how you can too. Roll around the room together – he'll think it's even more fun when Mum and Dad do it with him. You'll probably enjoy it too!

**7** to **10** months  mind  talking  moving  hands  friendliness

# ⑯ Baby's treasure trove

From about eight months when your baby's **manual dexterity** is really beginning to improve he'll love **looking inside** containers and discovering their contents. Create a special treasure trove of objects in a basket or cloth bag that he can **delve** into and **explore**.

## Bag of goodies

Collect together a selection of small, interesting objects, such as empty cotton reels, shells (check for sharp edges), pine cones, bricks and blocks in different shapes, balls, squeaky toys, rattles, cuddly toys, even items of clothing, such as socks or gloves. Put them all together inside an easy-to-open soft bag, such as a sponge bag or even a small pillow-case. Shake the bag so he can hear the contents moving about inside. Encourage him to feel the outside of the bag. Then help him open it and encourage him to unpack the contents for himself.

## Take and put back

Put a selection of items in a large basket. Sit your baby on the floor with the basket beside him and let him take the items out. Once they're all out on the mat help him to put them back again. This game helps his ability to let go as well as grasp items.

## Lucky dip

As before, only this time let him open the bag on his own and discover the contents. He'll love finding each item.

### Baby skills
that will benefit
from "Baby's treasure trove":
- *close observation* • *curiosity*
- *reasoning* • *concentration*
- *hand-eye co-ordination*
- *manipulation*
- *sorting*

**8** to **12** months ✓mind ✓talking moving ✓hands friendliness

# 8 to 9 months

The ninth month is a rewarding one because your baby's personality is really emerging. Watch as he

- initiates games and jokes – a sure sign that he's developing a sense of humour
- asserts his will because he has a mind of his own.

# Your baby is desperate to become mobile because there are so many things to see and explore. Now's the time to toddler-proof your home!

## m**o**v**i**ng

Your baby is beginning to discover that sitting up isn't enough – he has a strong urge to propel his body and to try to bring himself upright. His muscles have developed to the extent that he

• can **sit** for quite long periods – up to 10 minutes – before he gets tired

• can **lean forwards** without falling, although he can't lean sideways or swivel at the waist

• **won't give up** if he wants to reach an object – he'll try various ways of moving himself to reach it but he still over-balances

• may **roll over** to get to a sitting position and may move around this way

• may **try crawling movements** if you lie him on his tummy and ask him to come towards you; don't be surprised if he goes backwards though – his brain can't yet sort out the correct muscles to use for going forwards and backwards.

• may **pull himself to standing** in his cot or by holding on to furniture, but he flops down because he hasn't the balance or co-ordination to sit down in a controlled way.

### Pointing

*Pointing is an important **developmental milestone**. Control of the index finger is the first step towards mastering the very fine skill of bringing together the thumb and forefinger to nip or pinch small objects, which happens between 10 and 12 months. **Give him small objects** and raisins or cooked peas to pick up to practise his grip and hand-eye co-ordination.*

## TALKING

Your baby's vocalization now sounds much more like speech. This month he

• starts to **add new sounds** and consonants like "t" and "w"

• **uses sounds** in an attempt to imitate your speech

• **babbles with "meaning"** – his tone rises and falls in the rhythm and pattern of actual speech

• may say "Dada" more often when his Daddy is present than when he isn't – an indication that he's learning to **match words and meaning**

• **shouts** to attract your attention

• understands the meaning of "bye-bye".

## mind

He has a firm idea of who he is and how he fits into his world. So he

- is very good at **showing** what he doesn't like – he'll put his hands over his face to stop you from washing it or over his head to stop you brushing his hair
- will **look under** a cloth for a toy you have hidden there
- has a **longer concentration** span with toys he really likes
- **understands** when you want him to do something, such as holding out his hands to be washed.

## hands

Your baby's grasp is getting finer. His ability to handle small objects is improving and he demonstrates this perfectly when he

- tries to **turn over the pages of a book**, although he usually turns several at a time
- **points** very dramatically at everything he wants and makes imperious sounds to **indicate** his request
- **holds** a brick in each hand and can bang them together
- **explores toys** with his fingers more than with his mouth
- holds an object between his thumb and fingers
- "**rakes up**" small pieces of food, like raisins or peas, with his fingers and thumb.

# "pat-a-cake, pat-a cake"

## friendliness

Your baby's **personality** is emerging – he may be serene, a fusspot, noisy, determined, irritable, sensitive. Whatever he's like he

- **loves to join in** everything that you do, although he's quite good at playing on his own
- **enjoys playing** with you – rolling balls, batting balloons or playing "Pat-a-cake" – and **anticipates** actions
- understands when someone is going and may start to **wave** "bye-bye"
- enjoys having a **joke** and **teasing** games.

# *The* Golden Hour

By the end of this month he may be crawling – help him to achieve this **momentous event** with physical games and enthusiastic encouragement.

# "keep sharing jokes"

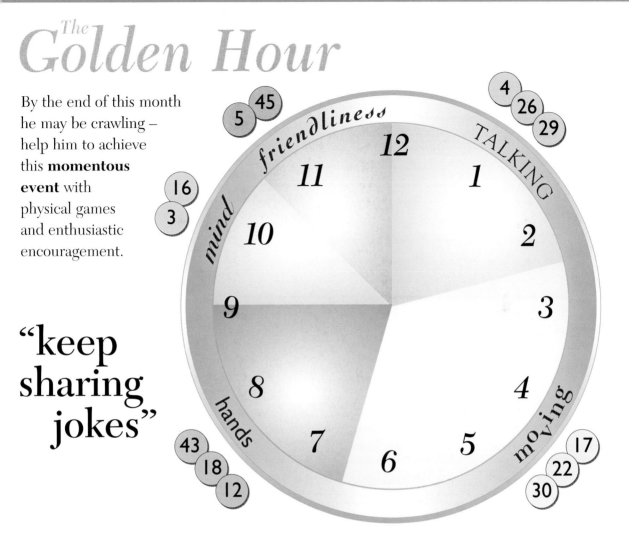

## TALKING

Keep saying, "Bye-bye" and waving your hand when someone's leaving. **Describe and demonstrate everything.**

## *friendliness*

Try some **co-operative games** like rolling a ball backwards and forwards, "Pat-a-cake", Incy-wincy spider and Peep-bo.

## hands

**Encourage him to point** at things by asking, "What do you want?" and "Show Daddy". Point at the pictures as you look at books together to **encourage him to copy**. Show him how to stack bricks one on top of the other because he can **release** his grasp now. Suitable props: **books, bricks**

## m°v¡ng

He's longing to propel himself – move toys away so he has to move to get them or sit yourself at a distance and hold out your arms to him. Now he's **very good at sitting**, sit on the floor with him to play. Encourage him to pull himself up by placing furniture that will give purchase and **hold him upright** yourself.

# ⑰ Tunnel fun

This game encourages **crawling** and **adventurousness**. Your baby may be a bit nervous at first, but he'll soon learn to enjoy navigating homemade tunnels, especially if you're waiting to give him a hug at the other end!

## Making the tunnel

The tunnel need only be short and makeshift. You can buy one from a toy shop, but you may find it's a bit long for a baby under a year. So just drape a sheet over two chairs set back to back a little way apart or use large cardboard boxes. You could also lay a cardboard box on its side, with both ends open. Make sure it's easy for your baby to back out of it.

**Baby skills**
that will benefit
from "Tunnel fun":
• *crawling* • *mobility*
• *curiosity* • *adventurousness*
• *determination* • *achievement*
• *concepts of "under"
and "through"*

### Two in a tunnel

Lie on your tummy beside your baby. Wriggle halfway through the tunnel, then turn round and invite him to join you. If he doesn't want to, don't force him. If he does, give him a big hug and talk to him, telling him he's in his and Mummy's secret den.

### Hidden treasure

Put a few tempting toys halfway down the tunnel and leave him to crawl towards them. Go to the other end and call him to you.

### All the way through

Put your baby at one end of the tunnel and sit at the other end. Encourage him to crawl all the way through and say, "Clever boy!"

### Mummy is the tunnel

Of course you don't need to make a tunnel at all. Get onto all-fours and make your body into a tunnel, then get your baby to crawl underneath you – or through your arms and legs. He'll love it!

---

*8* to *12* months   ✓ mind   ● talking   ✓ moving   ✓ hands   ✓ friendliness

# (18) Raisin trail

This game encourages **crawling** and is rewarding for your baby because each step on the trail yields something sweet and chewy (and healthy) to eat. It gets him to use his **forefinger to point** and then the **fine finger-and-thumb grasp** to pick up something small, like a raisin.

### Baby skills

that will benefit from "Raisin trail":
• pointing • pincer grip
• hand-eye co-ordination • hand control • close observation
• recognition • concentration
• looking till you find something

## 8-9 months

### Food for little fingers

Put lots of small items of food, such as raisins, peas or sweetcorn, in front of your baby on the tray of his highchair. Spread them out about 2 cm (1 in) apart so that he can see them clearly as separate items. Point to each type of food and name it. He probably won't be able to pick them up individually yet, but he'll try to scoop them up in his fist to eat. At this stage that's fine!

### Reach for a treat

Once he can sit up securely on the floor and swivel his body without falling over, sit him on a clean towel or blanket. Put raisins round him – some right behind him – so that he has to turn to reach them. Now put some just out of reach ahead of him so that he has to rock forward to get them.

## 9-12 months

### Snacks to go

The next step is to put the raisins about 40 cm (18 in) apart in a straight trail along the floor. Encourage him to shuffle or crawl to pick them all up.

### Racing for raisins

Once he's crawling confidently, make a wiggly trail of raisins for him to follow. Get down on all-fours and go round with him – have a race. He'll love it, especially when you let him beat you to the next raisin every time!

# 9 to 10 months

Your 10-month-old will be showing huge and rewarding enjoyment in all her activities. Also by this month she

- may well be sleeping through the night
- enjoys feeding herself
- will be good company.

## "Mama, Dada"

### *friendliness*

Your baby won't want to be left out of family activities now because she

- engages readily in all **social rituals** – greetings, goodbyes and mealtimes
- **loves being included** at the table for meals and will try to chime in the conversation to be part of the **social gathering**
- will bang a spoon to **attract your attention** or put her plate on her head to show off, but she'll begin to learn what's acceptable behaviour at table by following your example
- is proud of being able to **feed herself** while you eat.

And she's off! However she chooses to propel herself around there's no stopping her. Her keen sense of curiosity drives her onwards and upwards…

## m°v¹ng

Now your baby is really on the move and she
• can **pull herself up** to standing with ease, confidence and good balance
• **crawls or shuffles** on her bottom, pulling herself forwards with her hands, but her tummy may still not be completely off the floor when crawling
• may miss out crawling or shuffling altogether but however she moves, she's **confidently mobile** and moves forwards onto her hands and knees when she's sitting

• loves her **movement skills** – she'll roll over and over, get herself into a sitting position, pull herself to standing, then sit down again
• can nearly control the movement from standing to sitting without toppling over. She's **learning to balance** her body now because she
• is beginning to twist her trunk around in an **attempt to swivel**, but is still a bit unsure
• can move from her tummy to sitting up and from sitting up to lying on her tummy
• has perfect balance when seated.

## TALKING

She understands language as more than just vocal patterns. As proof of this new skill she
• **understands** the precise meaning of quite a few words, although she can't say any yet
• develops the word "Mama" soon after "Dada", which she **says more often** when Mummy's there than when she's not
• might begin to sound the **beginning of words** like "do" for "dog" – help her hear the "g" on the end of the word by emphasizing it with another syllable, as in "doggie", "horsey", "Mummy", "Daddy"
• may say **one word with meaning** by the end of this month, but don't worry if she doesn't, just *understanding* the meaning is more important for now.

## *mind*

Your baby enjoys showing off her understanding. See how she
• is becoming very **familiar with routines** and enjoys them
• puts her foot up when you hold out her sock and holds her hand up to go into the sleeve of her coat
• **waves** "bye-bye" when you say it
• knows her favourite soft toys and **pats and strokes** them when you say, "Nice Teddy"
• **remembers** the actions and rhythms of familiar rhymes and games all the way through
• **likes noisy toys** – she'll **examine** them closely and look for what is making the noise
• pulls your clothes to **attract your attention**.

# "where's Daddy?"

### Out in the car

*From this age you may find you need to **keep her amused** on long car journeys. Attach a tray to the car seat and give her a treasure box or bag with lots of interesting, safe items to discover, like cotton reels, squeaky toys, bricks and board books. Play some music and show her interesting things outside.*

## hands

Your baby will be able to do a lot more with her toys now that she
• reaches out for all small objects with her forefinger **guiding her hand** accurately to them
• has entirely mastered her fine grasp between finger and thumb and it's very **accurate**
• has excellent **hand-eye co-ordination** so she can pick up a small object with ease (but be careful what you leave lying around)
• loves **dropping and picking up** games now that she can release her grip – she'll drop toys endlessly from her highchair and she'll watch them fall; she knows exactly where they've gone even if they roll out of sight and she'll shout and point for you to pick them up again
• loves **rummaging** in bags and boxes and will repeatedly take things out and put them back.

# The Golden Hour

Everything is beginning to come together now – **intellectual skills** are helping her to understand language and be friendly. She's moving about quite freely and her hand-eye co-ordination is so skilled that she can **pick up small objects** by stooping.

## "keep asking simple questions"

## hands

The finest movement she'll ever learn – the **pincer grip** between thumb and forefinger – is perfected this month so give her small safe objects to pick up on her highchair tray or lay her a **raisin trail**. She now has enough **hand control** to let things go and put things down carefully so give her a treasure basket to sort. Suitable props: **basket, bricks**

## TALKING

She's **babbling away** so babble with her. Ask lots of simple questions and recite nursery rhymes to promote her **understanding of words**. Repeat her words, such as "dada" for Daddy, "doe-doe" for dog, but with meaning – say, "Yes, there's Daddy" or "Look at this picture of a dog." Suitable props: **books**

## mOving

She's so **good at crawling** you'll be worn out if you try to crawl at the same rate! Create play tunnels and play crawling chase games on your living room floor or out on the grass in the garden.

# (19) Obstacle course

These games **build confidence** and encourage your baby to use his whole body for **balance** and **flexibility** prior to **standing** and **walking**. To be able to move nimbly on all-fours and to get into a "crab" position so that he can stand up without a support, he has to **use his arms and legs** to manoeuvre his body. You'll find your baby is ingenious at discovering ways to get over and around things and will proudly show you his circumnavigating skills.

**SAFETY FIRST**
Make sure obstacles are soft, unlikely to fall over and not too tall. Stay with your baby while he negotiates the "course".

**Baby skills**
that will benefit from "Obstacle course":
• *mobility* • *confidence*
• *co-ordination* • *balance*
• *strength* • *crawling*
• *standing* • *walking*
• *discovery*

## Pillow mountains

Put a line of pillows on the floor with "barriers", such as a sofa and chairs on either side. Sit your baby at one end of the line and you sit at the other. Call his name and stretch out your arms. He'll come to you, but he might zigzag round the cushions. Repeat, but this time show him how to climb over them.

## Up and over

Make an obstacle course using cushions and other furniture. Make a circle of cushions, placing some on the floor and putting some over the sofa so that he's encouraged to climb up and down en route.

## On his feet

Sit on the sofa and encourage your baby to pull himself to standing holding on to the sofa. Then say "Sam stands up! Can Sam climb to Daddy? Aren't you clever?" Once he's confidently standing up and holding on to furniture, move to another seat, hold out your arms and encourage him to come to you.

**9** to **12** months  ✓mind  ● talking  ✓moving  ✓hands  ● friendliness

# ⟨20⟩ In the sandpit

The touch of sand is full of wonder for your baby. It teaches many concepts. It **pours** and **fills** and can be **emptied out**. If it's damp your baby can **make sand into pies or castles** and knock them down so he can start all over again. It has an advantage over water in that he won't get wet and spilt sand can easily be swept up. When you introduce him to sand, **describe and demonstrate all its features** – the tiny grains, how it can flow and stay in piles, what happens when it's damp and when it's dry.

## Baby skills

that will benefit from "In the sandpit":
- *sense of touch* • *hand-eye co-ordination* • *manipulation*
- *curiosity* • *experimentation*
- *concepts of full and empty*
- *construction* • *creativity*
- *imagination*

## Buckets of fun

Dampen the sand and make a row of sand pies using play beakers or a beach bucket – depending on the size of your sandpit. Count the pies and if you use stacking beakers describe the different sizes of the pies. Then let your baby knock them down – he'll love flattening them with his fists and palms. Build them up again and let him help you fill the beakers and pack in the sand.

## Sandy scene

Sand is similar to soil in that you can use it to create all kinds of things. Use some sand and toys to make an outdoor scene, such as a garden. You can put in play people and animals, make a house out of building bricks and add some pebbles, twigs, leaves and flowers.

### SAFETY FIRST

Use special play sand (available from toy shops and garden centres). Make sure your baby doesn't put sand in his mouth. If your sandpit is outside, make sure it has a secure cover so that cats can't get into it. If your baby gets sand in his eyes make sure he doesn't rub them. Gently tilt his head back and rinse out his eyes with cold water.

**9** to **12** months  ✓ mind   ✓ talking   moving   ✓ hands   friendliness

# 10 to 11 months

Physical and intellectual development at this age can vary enormously from one baby to another and still be perfectly normal. This is one of the times when you'll notice big differences between your baby and friends' babies of the same age. Nonetheless he

- probably hasn't started walking yet, but is practising early steps by lifting his leg while supported by you or holding on to the furniture – that's cruising.
- is beginning to look more like a child and less like a baby
- is growing very fast.

## TALKING

Although he may not be saying words yet you'll see that his understanding is positively exploding so he

- tries to say one or two **words with meaning** like dog or cat
- **points** to a duck in a picture if you ask, "Where's the duck?"
- tries to **make the noise** when you ask, "What does a duck say?"
- **nods or shakes his head** to indicate "Yes" and "No" to simple questions like "Do you want a drink?" or "Do you want more to eat?"

## *mind*

His understanding of concepts and his recognition skills are sharpening so that he

- **points** to familiar things in a book that he likes
- **understands** that the cat and kitten in his book, his toy kitten and Granny's cat are all cats, even though they're so different
- **enjoys playing games** that involve opposites – hot/cold, rough/smooth, round/square, big/little – especially if you act them out
- still has a **short attention span** when looking at books and will want to turn the pages quickly
- is **learning about cause and effect** – drop the brick and you pick it up, bang the drum and it makes a noise, shake the rattle and it rings a bell
- **enjoys** putting things into a container and taking them out and pouring water into and out of containers in the bath.

He's probably on his feet now and cruising. That all-important first step is a little way off, but he's perfecting his balance and co-ordination in readiness.

## Safety first

*Once your baby finds his feet be prepared for bumps and bruises and quickly comfort and reassure him when he **topples**. Cover sharp corners and check all furniture for stability. Try moving certain pieces to make it easier for your baby to **cruise freely**.*

## moving

Your baby is now striving to get upright most of the time and he
• practises lots of **pre-walking movements** tentatively so when he's standing holding on to the furniture or your hands, he'll lift his foot off the ground in a stepping movement and may stamp his foot a few times
• can **scamper about** swiftly on all fours if he's a crawler, with his tummy well clear of the floor
• can **lean over** sideways when sitting without toppling over
• can **twist his trunk** right round to reach something behind him and still keep his balance
• will **cruise around** the furniture by the end of this month to reach something or someone he particularly wants.

## Swimming with your baby

*Your 10-month-old baby is very active and needs to expend lots of energy, but it's difficult if space is limited or the weather keeps you indoors. Swimming is an* **excellent activity** *– babies usually love a pool if you introduce them to it gently. Many public pools offer exclusive times for parents, babies and toddlers to swim and you'll both* **enjoy splashing** *about in the water.*

# hands

The movements of his hands and fingers are really skilled and refined now. He
• can make his fingers **turn the pages** of a board book one at a time
• will put a brick into your hand if you ask for it and by the end of the month he'll **release** it into your hand – encourage this **give-and-take** by playing games and sharing rituals – "Let Mummy have one of your toast fingers. Thank you! Now you have a bit of Mummy's toast"
• will accurately **roll a ball** to you if you ask him, using his hands cleverly to make it roll with good aim
• starts to put bricks into shaped holes.

# *friendliness*

He's very helpful and wants to assist you in whatever you're doing. For example he
• will **imitate** your "housework" – he'll try to wipe his highchair tray if you give him a cloth
• will try to **help dress** himself or give you his nappy when you're changing him
• imitates you drinking tea, brushing your hair and cleaning your teeth
• **loves doing things together** – whether it's looking at books, going to the shops, lying on the bed or playing in the garden
• will **play happily** with another baby if they're put on the floor together.

# The Golden Hour

Your baby's understanding of what you say and the world around him is getting quite expert, even though he can only use a few words to express himself. He will show you he **wants to get involved** in whatever you're doing by trying to **copy you** so base some of the Golden Hour games around his urge to be included.

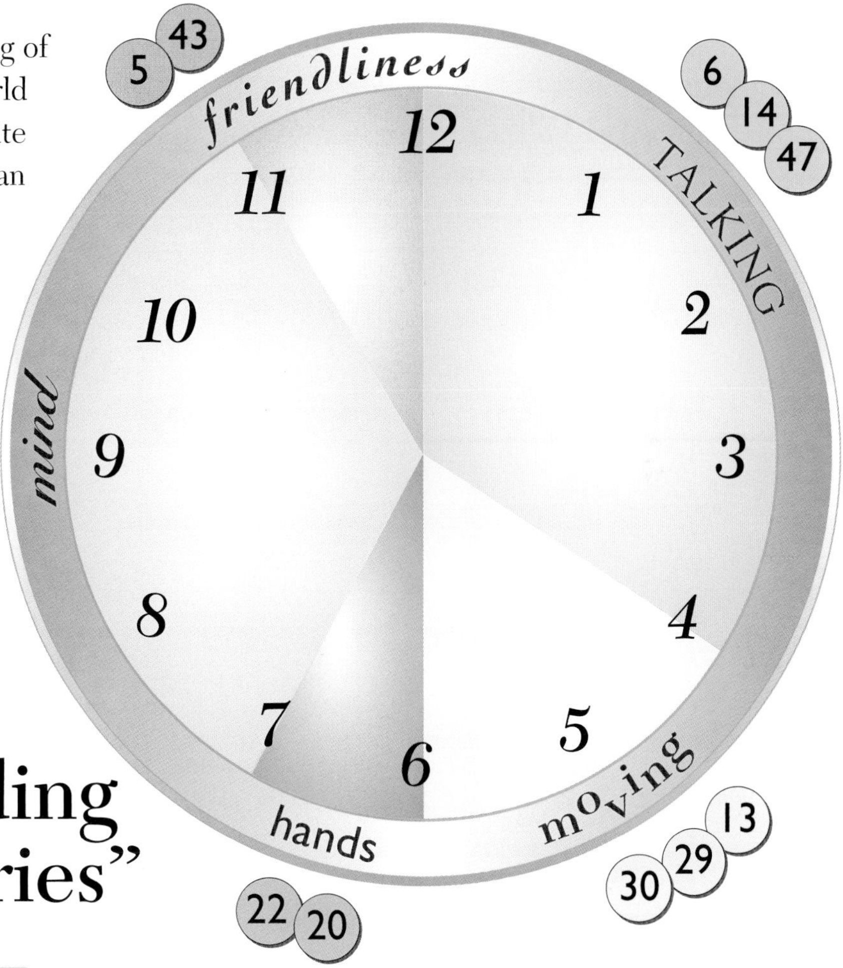

## "keep reading him stories"

*friendliness*

**TALKING**

*mind*

12 11 10 9 8 7 6 5 4 3 2 1

5 43 6 14 47 35 21 10

*moving*

hands

13 29 30 22 20

## TALKING

He can **nod and shake his head** so try to ask questions when you're doing everyday tasks and encourage him to answer you with gestures. Nod and shake your head as well so he can copy you – he's good at that now. He understands the concept of a simple storyline so tell him stories with actions to make it easy.

## mind

He's familiar with the idea of concepts, such as **opposites** and **cause and effect**. Water and sand games teach the concept of volume and the nature of liquids and solids. He can turn over pages so spend quiet times looking at books. Suitable props: **books**

## moving

Now he'll start to pull himself up and **cruise** round the furniture so help him with a treasure trail or an obstacle course or hold his hands to **encourage him to walk**. Be adventurous!

77

# ㉑ Matching and sorting

**Sorting like** from unlike is a difficult task even for an adult. **Matching** pairs and groups isn't entirely straightforward. But babies have the potential to acquire this basic skill in the first year. And it's important he does because it's the **basis of reasoning**, **decision making** and an essential first step to **reading**.

### Baby skills

that will benefit from "Matching and sorting":
• *matching* • *identifying differences* • *observation*
• *pattern recognition*
• *concentration*
• *reasoning*

### Animal groups

Find a book with big clear pictures of animals, especially adult and baby animals. Point out that cows, horses and dogs all have four legs, whereas birds have two, or that animals have fur and birds have feathers.

### Both the same

Point out the similarities between everyday objects: "Your cup and your spoon are both red." "This apple and this orange are both round."

### Shapes

Babies can spot differences in shape as long as they're clear. Cut out lots of shapes – triangles, squares, circles – and get your baby to match them.

### Post box

A posting box with different-shaped holes is a good toy as it encourages your baby's skill in matching shapes and his ability to manipulate the pieces into the right holes.

## (22) Hammering home

Hammering pegs requires many skills your baby acquires from eight months. A baby has to move his whole body to tap something, whereas an adult can use a much more refined movement to do something like drumming his fingers. To get that degree of **fine movement** a baby has to learn to use his shoulder, arm, wrist and hand first. So hammering is a **stepping stone** to **fine hand movements** of all kinds.

**Baby skills**
that will benefit
from "Hammering home":
• *grasp* • *hand-eye co-ordination* • *aim* • *strength*
• *co-ordination of shoulder, arm and hand*
• *spatial achievement*
• *creativity*

### Hand over hand

Put your hand palm down on a flat surface. Lay your baby's hand palm down over it. Put your other hand over his hand. He'll pat your hand with his free hand – then pull your lower hand out and cover his top one again. He'll take a while to get the hang of it, but it's a firm favourite.

### Peg table

Once his grasp is steady, try to obtain a special toy peg table and wooden hammer. Show your baby how to hammer the pegs into the holes. Then tell him it's his turn. He'll love copying you and will soon manage to hammer the pegs by himself.

### Getting the rhythm

Encourage banging movements by patting rhythms on your baby's highchair tray or on the floor. Get him to copy you.

### Making music

Give your baby a toy drum or a tambourine to bang. A simple xylophone or other musical percussion instrument will also provide hours of fun.

*8* to *12* months  ✔ mind • talking ✔ moving ✔ hands • friendliness

# 11 to 12 months

As your baby approaches her first birthday you can look back on the amazing strides she has made on all fronts. Where once she was helpless and weak, weighing just a few pounds, now she

- is strong enough to stand up and maybe even take a few steps
- feeds herself
- understands what you say and tries to talk
- loves jokes and joins in playing games with you.

# You've seen your precious newborn develop into a lively, sociable one-year-old. You've completed a magical first year as a family too – well done!

## One at a time

*At this stage so many skills are maturing simultaneously on the Baby Skill Map, it shouldn't surprise you if your baby surges ahead in one area and seems to stand still in another. If she's putting all her energy into learning to walk she hasn't much time to stop and talk. Conversely if she's starting to chat away and learn the names of things she may delay learning to walk for a while.*

## mind

You may not notice a huge difference in her behaviour between the 11th and 12th months, but there's lots going on. Now she

- can **follow** fast-moving objects with her eyes
- can **judge** the different sizes of objects from several feet away
- uses **memory** and experience to colour her reaction to things
- may start some simple forms of **fantasy play**, such as pretending to drink from a cup
- **listens** to very short stories all the way through
- is totally **fascinated** by books
- **experiments** with cause and effect – submerging a bath toy for it to bob up again.

## friendliness

Now she knows the power of her affections and will give them or withhold them for effect. For example she

- **kisses** on request, but won't if she doesn't feel like it
- **shows many emotions** especially **affection**, and will pat the dog, kiss Mummy or hug Daddy
- is apt to be shy with strangers but **loves family gatherings** and outings in the car or in her buggy
- **loves being in a crowd** especially with other children, but she'll hold on to you until she's confident enough to join in – even then she'll keep checking that you're close by and may cry if you leave the room unexpectedly.

## hands

Her wrist bones have grown so her hands are more manoeuvrable and she

• is much more accurate at getting food into her mouth with a spoon

because she's learned to **rotate her hand** to get the spoon between her lips

• has stopped mouthing everything she picks up – how an object **feels** in her hands is more important now

• is quite good at **throwing**

• can hold two bricks in one hand

• can **build** a tower of two blocks by placing one accurately on top of the other, thanks to her improved hand-eye co-ordination and steadiness

• will hold a crayon and may try to **scribble** if you show her how.

## m°v¹ng

Your baby may walk at the turn of her first year, but don't be surprised if she's as old as 18 months before she does, especially if she's an accomplished crawler. Around now she

• may develop a new way of crawling on her hands and feet with her legs extended like a bear – she's **halfway to walking**

• may **stand unaided** for a minute if you let go of her hands

• may take a **faltering step** and come to you if you call her name and encourage her to let go of the furniture – she **may launch herself** across gaps if you move furniture slightly further apart and so gain confidence to walk

• will walk if you hold just one of her hands

• will **push** a sturdy baby trolley across the floor for a few steps.

## TALKING

Now her speech is really going to take off and she

• can **say two or three words** with meaning and make **animal noises**

• starts "**jargoning**" – an imitation of what she hears you say to other people or an attempt to copy the running commentary you keep up when you're with her – you'll notice long **ramblings** of sound and here and there, the odd intelligible word

• has completely mastered "Yes" and "No" as nodding and shaking her head

• **understands** simple questions like, "Where's your shoe?" or "Where's your book?" and will search for them

• doesn't dribble much any more, a sign that she's **gaining control** over her tongue, mouth and lips **ready for speech**.

# The Golden Hour

She's nearly a toddler and the big milestones of **walking** and **talking** are here or fast approaching. These are such momentous achievements that other skills may take a back seat for a while.

## "keep helping her to make friends"

## moving

Help her to **stand alone** – hold her upright by her hands and then let go. Stay close by to catch her though! Get her to push along a sturdy trolley and walk with one hand. Push the pieces of furniture she cruises round further apart. She'll soon **launch off** on her own.

## TALKING

Encourage those **first words** that she uses with meaning by repeating stories with her, **repeating** nursery rhymes, call and response games, clapping games, music and puppet play. Suitable props: **book, puppet, tape**

## hands

Her **hand-eye co-ordination** is now so good she'll want to try **self-feeding** with a spoon. Allow her to and praise her when she succeeds. Don't mind the mess!

## friendliness

She **loves babies** of her own age so invite little friends **to play** and go to parent and toddler groups.

# ㉓ Kitchen percussion

This game satisfies your baby's innate desire to **bang** things and her love of **rhythmic noises**. And it's all so easy because there are so many objects she can use readily available in your kitchen cupboard – a wooden spoon in each hand or a pair of pan lids as cymbals to crash together. She'll learn to **recognize** low- and high-pitched notes by banging different materials and she'll learn to **use both hands** simultaneously.

**Baby skills**

that will benefit from "Kitchen percussion":
- *grasp* • *hand-eye co-ordination* • *hand control*
- *strength* • *creativity*
- *listening*

### Pots and pans

Pick a selection of safe kitchen items – pans, metal casserole dishes, wooden bowls, plastic boxes, biscuit tins – and put some upside down. Give her a wooden spoon or spatula and show her how to tap them. Describe and demonstrate, hold her hands and do it for her. Then see if she can do it herself.

### Cymbal clash!

Give her two fairly lightweight pan lids. Help her to clash them together like cymbals.

### Drumsticks

Put a plastic washing-up bowl upside down in front of her and bang it with different items, such as a wooden spoon, a metal spoon, a washing-up brush or a wire whisk. Describe the different sounds and encourage her to take over.

### Grand finale

Lay out a line of upturned pans and other items as before, but this time bang them in definite rhythms. Bash the kitchen orchestra together.

# ㉔ Paint magic

Let her be **creative** once she's getting good with her hands by introducing paint and **hand painting**. She'll love the chance of making a mess and **experimenting** with the texture and colour of paint with her fingers. Later, try some **printing** techniques with her and if her **manual dexterity** is advanced enough, show her how to use a **paintbrush**.

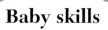

**Baby skills**

that will benefit from "Paint magic":
• *hand control* • *hand-eye co-ordination* • *cause and effect* • *experimentation* • *concept of colours* • *imagination*

## Exploring paint

Sit your baby in her highchair. Protect her clothes, roll up her sleeves and put newspaper or a plastic sheet under the chair. Pour a little non-toxic poster paint onto her highchair tray. Encourage her to "draw" with the paint using her finger. She'll soon get the idea and she may start using both hands to make a lovely mess!

## Colour trails

As the game above, but put more than one colour on the tray. Pour each new colour in each corner of the tray and see if she can use her finger to make trails of paint that join up. Don't be surprised though if it ends up as a great, messy mixture – she'll love it!

## Precious prints

When her hands are covered with paint (as they inevitably will be) show her how to print her palms onto a big piece of paper – you can keep one as a precious memento! When she's around 12 months try getting her to print. Use half-potatoes cut into interesting patterns or small sponges or pieces of rag.

## ㉕ Baby music

Research shows that children **love classical music** by composers such as Bach and especially Mozart – it stimulates the parts of the brain that are associated with maths and logic and helps **concentration** and **talking**. Choose music with a regular beat and classical harmonies, especially those incorporating string instruments. **Play music from birth** and never stop.

### Baby skills

that will benefit from "Baby music":
• *listening* • *sense of rhythm*
• *turning eyes and head to sound*
• *talking* • *handling emotions*
• *concentration* • *later –*
*mathematical and*
*logical thinking*

### Move to the beat

Hold your baby securely on your forearms and hands and with your face 20-25 cm (8-10 in) away, gently raise her up and lower her down in time to the music. Dads are especially good at this.

### Locating sound

Lay your baby in her cot and place a tape or CD player on one side of the room. Let her listen to the music for a while, then turn it off, move the player to the other side of the room and switch it on again. This will encourage your baby to turn her head towards the sound.

### Time to relax

Try to choose the same time each day to put on some music. Make sure your baby is fed, clean and dry, then lie down with her on your chest. Pat or stroke her back in time to the music.

# (26) Songs and lullabies

Babies love to be sung to, especially by you. It's **soothing**. They also feel they're the centre of attention, which gives them **security** and a sense of importance – crucial for **self-esteem**. At night a song is the best prelude to **contented** sleep and makes for **happy** bedtimes – every child's birthright.

And remember any song sung slowly can be a lullaby, even if it's the latest hip-hop track from the charts!

### Baby skills

that will benefit from "Songs and lullabies":
• *talking* • *listening*
• *responding to music*
• *memory* • *friendliness*
• *rhythm*

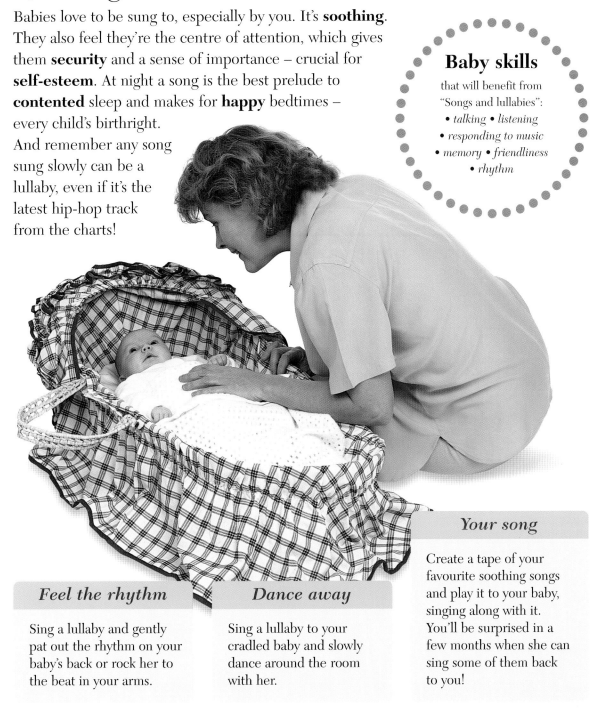

### *Feel the rhythm*

Sing a lullaby and gently pat out the rhythm on your baby's back or rock her to the beat in your arms.

### *Dance away*

Sing a lullaby to your cradled baby and slowly dance around the room with her.

### *Your song*

Create a tape of your favourite soothing songs and play it to your baby, singing along with it. You'll be surprised in a few months when she can sing some of them back to you!

---

**0** to **12** months   ✔ mind    ✔ talking    moving    hands   ✔ friendliness

## Baby skills

that will benefit from
"Action nursery rhymes":
• *talking* • *listening*
• *responding to music* • *memory*
• *friendliness* • *rhythm*
• *co-ordination*
• *anticipation*

## ㉗ Action nursery rhymes

Nursery rhymes help your baby learn to talk as they mimic the rhythm of speech and **reinforce learning** by repetition. So from birth nurse and carry your baby while singing nursery rhymes. From about three months he'll learn the **actions** that go with the nursery rhymes and will be able to **anticipate** them as he becomes older and more co-ordinated.

### Choosing rhymes

Build up a repertoire of nursery rhymes (look up the old favourites in books to remind yourself of the words) and sing the same ones over and over. Your favourites will become your baby's favourites and he'll enjoy the repetition.

### Name change

Substitute your baby's name in a song he knows, such as "Sam and Jill went up the hill...". He'll be thrilled.

### What next?

Nursery rhymes can help your baby to understand the concept of a story, of what's coming next. Using a nursery rhyme tell the story with actions, gestures and emotion. Then when your baby knows them, pause at a crucial point and see if he can join in with the appropriate gesture. If he doesn't, then do it for him – it's only a game. "Guess what happens next. Yes! Little Miss Muffet sat on a tuffet. And then? Then came a spider and sat down beside her!" and so on.

**0** to **12** months mind talking moving hands friendliness

## 28 Shake, rattle and roll

Babies love lots of **different sounds**. When your baby is very young he'll prefer high-pitched sounds so squeaky toys are best. Later on anything goes! And he'll **enjoy** making the sounds themselves, whether it's with rattles and squeaky toys or his own vocalizations.

The rattle teaches a highly intellectual concept – **cause and effect** – "When I shake this rattle I **cause** it to make a noise."

**Baby skills**

that will benefit from "Shake, rattle and roll":
• *hand control* • *hand-eye co-ordination* • *grasping* • *cause and effect* • *hearing*

### 2-6 months

### Shake the rattle

Choose a rattle with a distinctive sound. Rattle it yourself so your baby can see and hear what you're doing. Describe and demonstrate. Tap the rattle on his hand gently, then curl his fingers round the handle. Place your hand over his and wave the rattle together. He'll soon have the strength to hold the rattle himself and shake it.

### 6-10 months

### Sit and squeak

Put a squeaky toy on a chair or on the floor. Show your baby what you're doing, then sit on it to make it squeak: "Oops, silly Mummy!" Laugh with your baby. Sit your baby on a squeaky toy and take turns to make it squeak.

### Big squeeze

Squeeze a squeaky toy to make it squeak, then take your baby's hand and help him do it. Squeezing is quite difficult so he'll take a while to master it on his own.

### Find the noise

Put a soft squeaky toy onto the changing mat and lay your baby gently on top so the toy squeaks. Ask him, "Where did that noise come from?" Find the toy and squeak it again. Repeat as often as you want.

## 29 Feet and toes

Feet and toes are just as interesting to your baby as her hands and fingers. From about four months she'll discover how to **catch hold of her feet** when she's lying on her back and she'll **play with her toes** with as much **interest** as her fingers. These games are for feet and toes and they make her more aware of her feet – an early **prelude to walking**.

### Baby skills

that will benefit
from "Feet and toes":
• *friendliness* • *humour*
• *feelings and emotions*
• *talking* • *imitation*
• *mobility*
• *co-ordination*

### This little piggy

Play this to demonstrate your baby's toes:
This little piggy went to market (*wiggle the big toe*)
This little piggy stayed at home (*wiggle the second toe*)
This little piggy had roast beef (*wiggle the third toe*)
This little piggy had none (*wiggle the fourth toe*)
And this little piggy (*wiggle the little toe*) went wee-wee-wee all the way home (*tickle your baby all the way up her leg and under her arm – or just tickle the sole of her foot*).

### Hob, shoe, hob

Lay your baby on her back and pat her bare feet in time to this rhyme:
Hob, shoe, hob; hob, shoe, hob
Here a nail, there a nail, that's well shod.

### Wee Wiggie

Count your baby's toes with this rhyme.
Wee Wiggie (*wiggle the little toe*)
Poke Piggie (*wiggle the fourth toe*)
Tom Whistle (*wiggle the middle toe*)
John Gristle (*wiggle the second toe*)
and old BIG GOBBLE, gobble, gobble!
(*pretend to eat up her big toe!*)

# ㉚ Horsing around

Your baby will love the rough and tumble of "riding" games. They develop her **balance** and **strength**, build **trust** between her and you and appeal to her **sense of adventure**. They also help to build her **knowledge** of horses and what makes them different from say, dogs and cats.

### Baby skills

that will benefit from "Horsing around":
- *balance* • *co-ordination*
- *strength* • *kicking*
- *understanding*
- *trust*

## The way the ladies ride

Once your baby can bring her head in line with her body when sitting she'll enjoy this rhyme. Hold her in a sitting position facing you on your knee:
This is the way the ladies ride
Trit-trot, trit-trot, trit-trot
(*"trot" your baby up and down*)
This is the way the gentlemen ride
Gallopy, gallopy, gallopy
(*"gallop" your baby up and down*)
This is the way the farmers ride
Galumph, galumph, galumph
(*wobble her from side to side*)
And DOWN into the ditch
(*pretend to "drop" her by lowering her quickly off your knee, but still hold her firmly*).

## Ride a cock horse

Sit your baby on your knee. Give her a rattle to shake during this rhyme:
Ride a cock horse to Banbury Cross
(*gently rock your baby up and down*)
To see a fine lady upon a white horse
With rings on her fingers and bells on her toes
(*encourage your baby to shake the rattle in time to the rhythm*)
She shall have music wherever she goes.

**4** to **12** months ✔mind ✔talking ✔moving ✔hands ✔friendliness

## ㉛ Play bracelets

Young babies lack co-ordination so their movements appear purposeless. Encourage him to **move his arms and legs**, thereby gaining **strength, control** and **purpose** by attaching a bell or a balloon to his wrist or ankle. He'll soon realise he can **make a sound** when he moves so he's learning about **cause and effect** as well as movement.

### *Fun with balloons*

Tie a small helium-filled balloon to your baby's wrist loosely with ribbon. Make sure the ribbon is long enough so the balloon is well out of reach. Help your baby move his arms so that he sees the balloon bob up and down. Then leave him to do it for himself.

### Baby skills

that will benefit
from "Play bracelets":
• *cause and effect*
• *concentration* • *seeing*
• *listening* • *mobility*
• *co-ordination*

### *Ring the bell*

Make or buy a "foot bracelet" with lightweight bells – the sort you might have on a cat's collar – threaded onto ribbon or soft elastic. Tie the bracelet to your baby's ankle. While he's lying on his back show him that with every kick the bells will ring. Do it several times, describing what happens. Then let him lie quietly for a few minutes. He'll move his legs involuntarily at some point and will learn that he can make the bells ring.

**SAFETY FIRST**
Never leave your baby
alone with a balloon.
If the balloon bursts
he could choke or
suffocate on
the pieces.

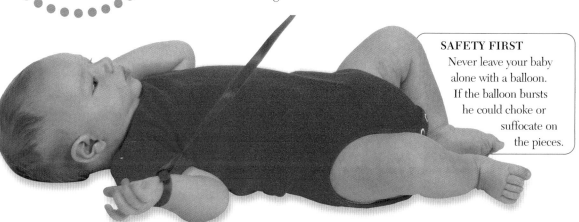

**2** to **6** months ✓ mind ● talking ✓ moving ✓ hands ● friendliness

## ㉜ Tissue paper fun

Anything lightweight and compressible is great fun for your baby because he can **see, hear** and **feel** the effect of his **actions**. Tissue paper can easily be **scrunched, torn** and **thrown** (make sure he doesn't just eat it!) and the rustling sound appeals to his **acute hearing**. A baby gets an idea of **intent** from what he learns each time he handles some tissue paper, and as it's so easy to handle he'll develop his skills very quickly.

### Baby skills

that will benefit from "Tissue paper fun":
• *cause and effect* • *hand-eye co-ordination* • *hand control* • *hearing* • *grasp* • *leg strengthening*

*2-5 months*

### Scrunch and kick

Scrunch up some tissue paper and put it at the end of his cot so that when he kicks he'll feel it and hear the rustling. Show him where it is and encourage him to kick.

### Show and tell

While he's sitting in his baby chair scrunch and rustle tissue paper so that he can see what you're doing. Explain and demonstrate. Describe the noise that the tissue paper makes.

*5-9 months*

### Tissue balls

Sit on the floor with your baby. Put piles of different coloured sheets of paper on the floor. Scrunch, tear and smooth out the paper, describing what you're doing. Then put a big ball of tissue into his hands and help him squeeze it.

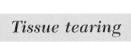

### Tissue tearing

As above, but tear sheets of tissue into strips. Show your baby how to start tearing – he'll need to use both hands.

## �33 Puppet play

From as early as eight weeks when your baby has mastered **focusing** her eyes and has achieved binocular vision (both eyes working together), she'll enjoy **simple games** with puppet figures. **Glove** and finger puppets are good for younger babies because they're soft and safe. **Wooden-spoon** puppets are ideal for older babies as they can be safely played with and banged. You can buy both glove and finger puppets, but they are also easy to make.

**Baby skills**

that will benefit from "Puppet play":
- *understanding* • *memory*
- *curiosity* • *observation*
- *concentration* • *imagination*
- *manipulation* • *participation*
- *talking* • *humour*

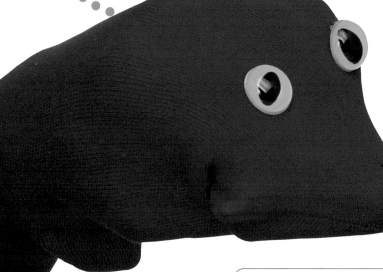

### Animal magic

Babies love animals so introduce a cuddly glove puppet such as a cat or dog. Show your baby the puppet, make the relevant animal noise, then show your baby a picture of a cat or dog or point out a real one. Describe and demonstrate: "Cats go miaow."

### Game for a laugh

Using your glove puppet play tickling games or Peep-bo.

### Rhyme time

Use finger puppets to act out simple nursery rhymes like Jack and Jill or Two little dickie birds. Help your baby to put the finger puppets on her own fingers.

### Wooden tops

Give your baby wooden-spoon puppets to play with. Make up stories and act them out using the puppets.

**SAFETY FIRST**
Check for small items that could become detached from the puppet and swallowed if it's chewed. If you buy your puppet check that it carries the CE safety mark.

**2** to **12** months  ✔ mind    ✔ talking    moving    ● hands    ✔ friendliness

# ㉞ Making simple puppets

Puppets make **versatile** playthings (see Activity 33) even for young babies and they're **simple to make** out of everyday

household items. You don't have to be good at sewing or crafts and because you can make them with throwaway items, it doesn't matter if they're not durable.

## You will need

• *felt* • *scissors*
• *glue*
• *fabric pens*

## Sock puppets

You can make very versatile glove puppets out of old socks. You don't even have to decorate them – simply push your fingers into the toe end and use your thumb to create the lower jaw of the puppet's mouth. But you can make a very simple face by sewing on buttons for eyes and nose or drawing them on with fabric pens.

**SAFETY FIRST**
Always use non-toxic paints and glues. Don't allow your baby to put these puppets in her mouth.

## Wooden-spoon puppets

Take any clean wooden spoon and paint a design on the spoon end with non-toxic paints. This could be a funny face or an animal or insect.

## Finger puppets

Very simple finger puppets can be made by cutting the fingers off old gloves, finishing the edges and decorating them appropriately. You can make more elaborate finger puppets as follows:

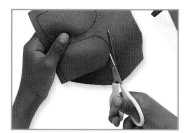

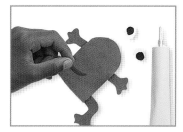

**1** Using your fingers to gauge the size of the finger puppet, mark out and cut two body pieces from a piece of brightly coloured felt or other fairly stiff fabric.

**2** Spread a fine line of glue round the edge of one body piece leaving the bottom edge free. Firmly stick the two pieces together. Leave to dry.

**3** Glue on features made from felt or draw them on with fabric pens. If you wish, you can also add limbs and tails to create simple, but recognizable animals.

## (35) Fun with dough

Babies love **materials** that they can **handle** – water, food, sand and dough. Dough's special appeal is that once moulded it keeps its shape. It's stretchy and sticky, can be rolled and kneaded and is colourful too. It also teaches many **intellectual ideas** that would be difficult to learn otherwise and encourages **fine finger and hand movements**. Dough can be bought commercially, but it's very easy and cheap to make your own.

### Baby skills

that will benefit from "Fun with dough":
- *hand control* • *finger control*
- *hand-eye co-ordination* • *imitation*
- *manipulation* • *concentration*
- *spatial awareness*
- *creativity* • *imagination*
- *cause and effect*

### Cat's whiskers

Roll out your dough and cut out a big cat shape (or any other animal) for your baby to look at. Make eyes, a nose, a mouth and some big whiskers and ask him where they should go. See if he can point to the right place. Stick them on and describe and demonstrate all the time.

### Dough man

Make a human figure with dough. You don't have to be a great artist to do this – your baby will recognize the basic shape! Put the dough man in various positions – sitting, hands on knees, doing a handstand, lying on his back, kicking or whatever. Describe and demonstrate. Let your baby poke and pull the figure if he wants to.

### Shaping up

Give your baby some dough, a toy rolling pin and some plastic pastry cutters and show him how to pound and roll the dough and to cut out shapes. Describe and demonstrate.

### Little pastry chef

Find a simple recipe for cheesy pastry or gingerbread biscuits. Let your baby help with the mixing, rolling out and cutting. Make a gingerbread man with currants for eyes, nose and mouth. There's bound to be a mess, but his enjoyment is more important than a bit of spilt flour! He'll love eating the end results and he'll learn so much about cause and effect in the meantime.

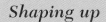

## ㊱ Making dough

All children love making things even if it's only mud pies. They see you cooking and doing other chores and even as early as eight or nine months they use pretend play to experiment with the skills they need to copy what you're doing. Dough provides an ideal material because of its plasticity, staying power and re-usability.

### *How to make dough*

Mix together 2 cups of flour, 1 cup of salt, 1 teaspoon of cream of tartar, 2 tablespoons of oil and 1 teaspoon of food colouring with 2 cups of water in a saucepan over a medium heat. Stir constantly until the dough comes together. Continue to stir for a couple of minutes, then take it out and knead it for several minutes. Keep it in an air-tight plastic container.

### **You will need**

- *flour* • *salt* • *oil*
- *water* • *cream of tartar*
- *food colouring*

### *Involving your baby*

Dough is participative. It doesn't matter what you're making, your baby can play with dough and make something himself by trying to imitate what your hands are doing. When you cook with pastry, always give a small piece to your baby to squeeze and shape. He feels grown up and valued because he's making a contribution and so are you. And when he's made a shape make sure you cook it for him too!

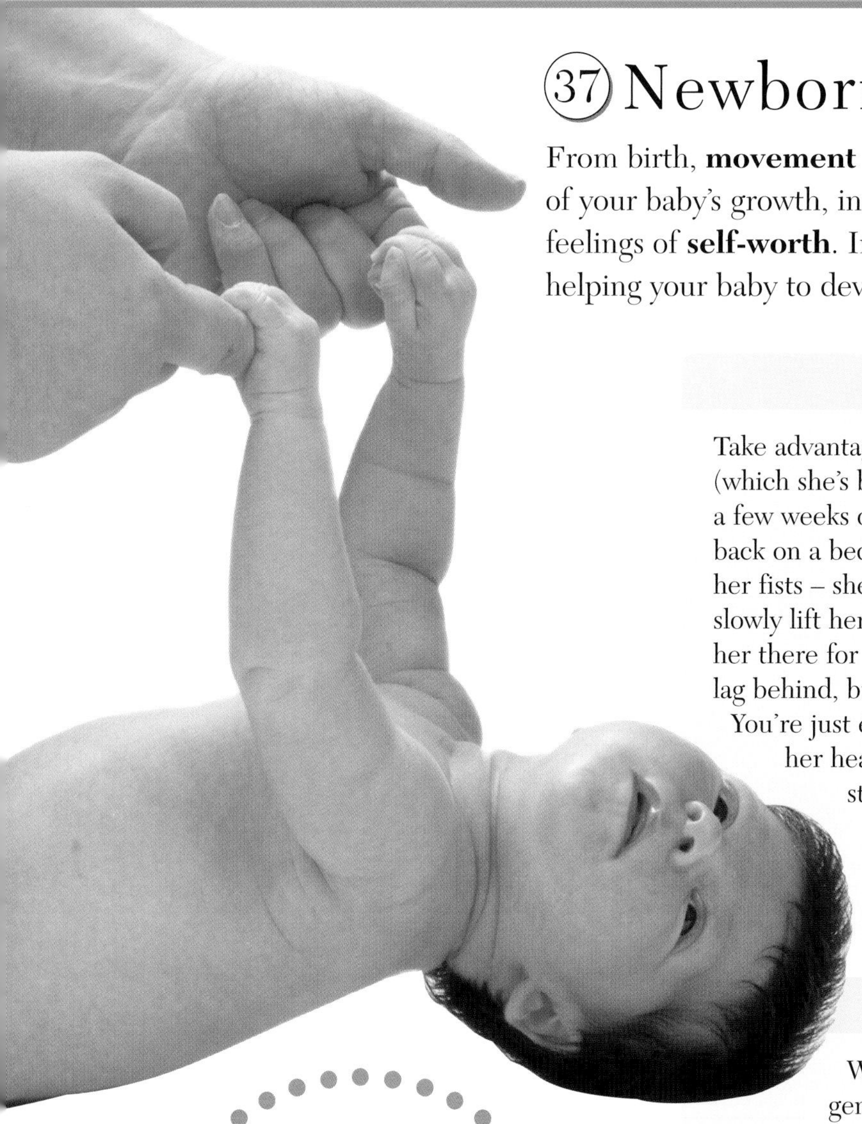

# �37 Newborn baby jig

From birth, **movement games** encourage every area of your baby's growth, including the **intellect** and feelings of **self-worth**. In addition you can begin helping your baby to develop **head control.**

## *Gentle lifts*

Take advantage of your baby's grasp reflex (which she's born with and keeps until she's a few weeks old). When she's lying on her back on a bed, place your index fingers into her fists – she will grip them tightly. Very slowly lift her a few centimetres and hold her there for a few seconds. Her head will lag behind, but she'll come to no harm. You're just encouraging her to try to hold her head in line with her body, which strengthens her neck muscles and helps head control. Lower her down gently – show her how clever she is.

## *Legs straight*

When she's lying on her back, gently uncurl her legs. At first her legs will stay curled in the fetal position and the sooner you help her learn to uncurl them, the sooner she'll start to kick and strengthen them. Praise her. After uncurling her legs very gently bend them at the knees a few times to loosen them. Uncurl her arms too.

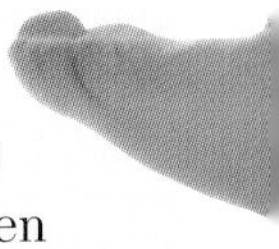

## Baby skills

that will benefit from "Newborn baby jig":
• *head control* • *movement awareness* • *bone, muscle and joint development* • *strength and mobility* • *developing brain-muscle-nerve connections* • *sense of achievement and fun*

---

**0** to **2** months  ✓mind  •talking  ✓moving  ✓hands  ✓friendliness

# ㊳ Floor flying

Your baby will enjoy lying on the floor with plenty of space around her, especially if you get down on the floor with her. It helps her to be more adventurous both physically and emotionally. **Wriggling** and **kicking** prepares her for **crawling** and all the effort she puts into learning to lift her body off the floor is made worthwhile when she realises she's **learning to propel herself**.

## Ready for take-off!

Lie on the floor on your tummy, head to head with your baby, about 15 cm (6 in) apart. Spread her arms out sideways like an aeroplane (explain what you're doing) and do the same yourself. Now raise your head and call her name. Praise her efforts to lift her head to look at you.

## Sky-diving

Lie side by side with your baby. Spread her and your arms outwards again and this time raise your legs as well, as if you were sky-diving. Encourage her to do the same. Praise her with a cuddle when you're both doing it.

**Baby skills**
that will benefit from
"Floor flying":
• *neck strength • head control • mobility • balance • rolling over • sitting • crawling • meeting challenges*

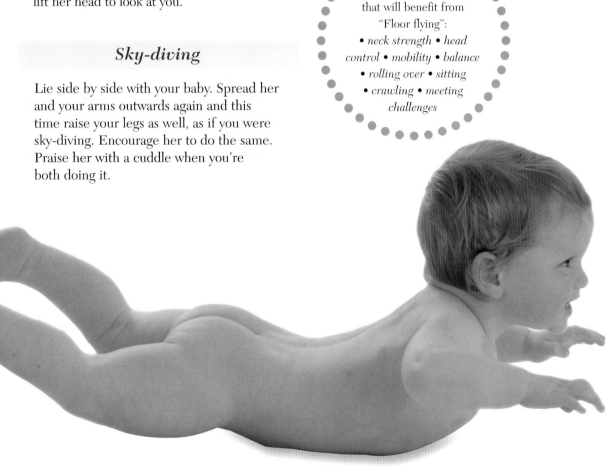

*4* to *8* months   ✔ mind   ● talking   ✔ moving   ● hands   ● friendliness

# ㉟ Baby sit-ups

You don't have to wait for perfect head control to play these games. It doesn't matter if his head hangs back, he'll try to hold it in line with his body and that effort **strengthens his neck**. Believe it or not this is the first step on your Baby's Skill Map for **walking**. And your baby will love being pulled up to a sitting position so that he can **look around.**

### Baby skills

that will benefit from "Baby sit-ups":
• *head control* • *sitting*
• *balance* • *mobility*
• *achievement* • *strength*
• *curiosity*
• *participation*

## *Up you come!*

Lay your baby on his back and then pull him up to a sitting position by holding his hands. Do it very slowly and gently so that even if his head lags it is not jerked roughly at any stage. Describe what you're doing as he gradually comes upright. Support him firmly as he sits upright for a minute or two, then lower him down onto his back again. His head control will improve week by week until at about four months he'll be able to keep his head in line with his body as you pull him upright.

## *Up and down*

Once he's beginning to hold his head in line with his body, sit him on your knee and bounce him up and down gently saying, "John's going up, John's going down."

## *Watch out!*

Once your baby can hold his head in line with his body (from four months), bounce him on your lap. Then holding him steady under his armpits, open your legs a little as if he's going to slip through.

---

 *1* to *6* months   ✓mind   talking   ✓moving   hands   friendliness

# ㊵ Baby gym

Before your baby can sit he spends a lot of waking time lying on his back in his cot or confined to a push chair or baby chair. You can **keep him happy** by providing a baby gym – a selection of **visually interesting** toys and objects (choose ones that make a noise too) strung safely across his cot where he can see them and later where he can **swipe at them**. This gym is special because as well as **exercising his arms** it exercises his **brain**. You can buy ready-made baby gyms, but you can also create your own simply by tying a variety of objects to cord or elastic.

### Baby skills
that will benefit from "Baby gym":
• *concentration* • *understanding*
• *seeing* • *focusing*
• *hand-eye co-ordination*
• *cause and effect*

## 0-3 months
### Good to touch

Shake the support so that the objects move. Touch each item in turn and describe what happens. Then take one of your baby's hands and help him reach up to touch the object. Then encourage him to try by himself.

### High kicks

Move the baby gym down to his feet and show him how to kick the objects.

## 3-6 months
### Grabbing and pulling

Use a baby gym with a rigid frame and items he can grab safely, like rings. Pull the rings so he can see what you're doing. Then put his hands into them and help him pull them himself. He'll soon learn to grab them.

**SAFETY FIRST**
For a homemade gym, use materials that don't tear when pulled and that are too big to go in your baby's mouth. Tie them firmly.

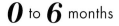 **0** to **6** months     ✓ mind     talking     ✓ moving     ✓ hands     friendliness

## ㊶ Baby ball games

These games aren't designed to get your baby into the national football team. The idea is to introduce him to the **concept of balls** and ball games. He may never play a game of tennis but ball games nonetheless confer many valuable physical skills, such as **hand-eye co-ordination** – a very important first-year skill to master. Start with simple air-filled balloons and then progress to a big, soft, bouncy ball.

### Baby skills

that will benefit
from "Baby ball games":
- *kicking • pushing • rolling*
- *hand-eye co-ordination*
- *timing • aim • hand control*
- *shape recognition*
- *taking turns*
- *sharing*

*4-7 months*

### Bouncing balloon

Prop your baby in his seat on the floor and bounce a balloon against his legs. Show him how to kick his legs to make it bounce back. A balloon is fun and introduces the concept of roundness.

### Kick it back

This needs two people and your baby. One person supports him sitting on the floor. The other rolls a balloon for him to kick or bat back.

*7-12 months*

### See the ball roll

Sit your baby on the floor and roll a big, colourful, bouncy ball gently towards his legs. Encourage him to kick or roll it back to you. Before he's a year old he'll have sufficient balance and hand control to intercept the ball with his outstretched arms or between his legs and to throw or roll it back to you. Every time you roll the ball don't forget to tell your baby, "The ball is rolling because it's round."

## (42) Baby press-ups

Your baby's ability to lift his head up when lying on his tummy is an **important step** on his Skill Map towards **crawling** and then **walking**. These simple physical games are a slow build up to more complicated skills. He won't be able to crawl if he can't sit up. He won't be able to sit up if he hasn't the strength to hold up his head (the heaviest part of his body for several months). And he won't be able to sit up steadily if he can't **balance his body** as he twists.

### 2-4 months
### *Head lifts*

Sit on the floor with your baby lying on his tummy facing you. Make sure his arms are spread out wide in front of him until he's strong enough to do this himself. Call his name and shake a rattle or wave a coloured toy about 20-25 cm (8-10 in) from his face. Hold it a little bit higher so that he has to try to raise his head to look at it. Praise him when he does so.

### 4-6 months
### *Off the floor*

Once he can lift his chest off the floor, hold the rattle further away and higher. Shake it to the right and left to encourage him to move his head from side to side.

### 6-9 months
### *Look behind*

Your baby has the strength to hold himself up with his weight on his hands only and his chest and tummy off the floor, with his head upright. Now get him to turn his whole body by shaking the rattle behind him. By nine months he'll reach for the toy with one hand and still keep his balance.

### Baby skills

that will benefit from "Baby press-ups":
• *head control* • *neck, back and arm strength*
• *mobility* • *rolling over*
• *balance*

**2** to **9** months ✓ mind ● talking ✓ moving ● hands ● friendliness

## 43 Give and take

Once your baby is able to grasp with all her fingers – at about 7-8 months – rather than her flat, open palm you can start to guide her to **refine her grasp** even further. Give and take games help her learn to **let go** of objects **on purpose** and **accurately** rather than just dropping them indiscriminately. Learning to give something to another person requires **social skills** too – it's the prelude to that most difficult lesson, **learning to share**.

### Baby skills
that will benefit from "Give and take":
- *hand-eye co-ordination*
- *hand control* • *finger control*
- *grasp refinement*
- *letting go* • *sharing*
- *observation*

---

*7-9 months*

### Give and take

Put a toy in the palm of her hand. When she's holding it say, "Mummy take it back for a second." Gently slip it out of her hand, then say, "Clever girl, you give it to Mummy." Big kiss. "So, Mummy will give it back to Lucy." Repeat.

### Lend a hand

Put a toy on her highchair tray and place her fingers on top of it so she can curl them round. Get her to try to pick it up.

### Get a grip

Slide a toy between her thumb and forefinger. She may use other fingers to hold it, but if you start it off in her thumb and fore-finger it helps to introduce the idea of the pincer grip.

*9-12 months*

### Learn to share

Give your baby a toy or small object that you know she hasn't seen before or hasn't played with recently. She'll be curious about it and keen to hold and explore it. Ask her to give it back to you. If she does, praise her and give the toy back to her. If she can't (or won't) give it back, take it from her gently, thanking her all the time and saying, "There's a good girl."

---

**7** to **12** months ✓mind ● talking ● moving ✓hands ✓friendliness

## ㊹ Family favourites

Babies **respond to voices** from birth. Your voice is so important to her that she's learned to distinguish it from all others by the time she's two weeks old. When she hears your voice she **feels secure**. Later she'll respond to **familiar faces** like those of other family members close to her – especially if they carry a smile! Family photos teach her that her Granny and Grandad exist even when they're not there and teach her the concept of family.

**Baby skills**

that will benefit from "Family favourites":
• *recognition* • *listening*
• *memory* • *talking*
• *forming relationships*
• *feeling secure*

### Familiar voices

Record your voice onto a cassette tape, just talking to your baby and saying her name or reading rhymes and poems. Make one tape of Mum's voice and another of Dad's. If your baby has other regular carers make a tape of their voices too. Settle your baby in her cot or pram, pat her gently and put on the voice tape. After a few minutes stop patting while the tape plays on.

### Familiar faces

Make a family album for your baby. Stick photographs of her loved ones onto card and let her study them. If possible make enlarged copies so that she can see them clearly. Talk about the people who are in the photographs.

### Learning to settle

Settle your baby, play the voice tape (see above) and walk away. If she protests go to her, turn off the tape and say her name. Then turn the tape on and leave again. This teaches your baby that you'll return if she needs you.

## ㊺ Baby massage

Almost 50 years ago research revealed that babies want to be **touched** as much as they want to be fed. To a newborn baby touch is as **essential as vitamins** to ensure he thrives. He'll always love gentle massage and it's never too early to start. So spend a few minutes a day concentrating on **touching all parts of his body** – it's heaven for him as well as making him aware of his whole body.

**Baby skills**
that will benefit
from "Baby massage":
• *forming relationships*
• *learning to trust* • *relaxation*
• *serenity* • *being responsive*
• *mobility*

### Naming body parts

Using both hands massage his face and head, starting in the middle of his forehead. As your baby grows and his understanding develops, always name the parts of the body as you massage. For example, as you massage his face draw attention to his eyes, nose and mouth and name them.

### Varying strokes

Lay your baby on his back and gently stroke his neck, shoulders, trunk, legs and feet, downwards from head to foot. Repeat very lightly and then again more firmly.

### Varying the pace

Repeat these strokes but this time very slowly, then very quickly. Describe what you're doing as you stroke him. Repeat these strokes when he's lying on his tummy.

### Using oil

Repeat all the previous strokes, but using a little baby oil rubbed onto your hands.

**0** to **12** months  mind  talking  moving  hands  friendliness

### Who's who?

Hold your baby in front of a mirror so he can see you and himself. Say, "That's Sam's face in the mirror" and stroke it gently. Then with a big smile point to your own face and say, "This is Mummy's face and she's smiling."

### Disappearing act

To help him understand that things go on existing even when he can't see them, show him your face in the mirror, then move so he can't see it there any more and then reappear. Accompany this with a running commentary, "There's Daddy, now he's gone, now Daddy's come back."

### What's what?

Point to your baby's eyes in the mirror and then on his own face: "Eyes see," then his ears, "Ears hear" and his mouth, "Mouths eat and smile and talk." Repeat, pointing to your own.

# ㊻ Mirror, mirror

From birth to the age of one year – and beyond – your baby is **fascinated by faces** and especially by how they're reflected in a mirror. Looking in the mirror is fun, but it's also a **highly intellectual** activity. At first he sees the mirror as simply a basic attachment to the human face. Then he's **curious** about who is behind the mirror. Then there's a dawning **recognition** that it's himself – very advanced!

**Baby skills**
that will benefit from "Mirror, mirror":
• *recognizing faces* • *recognizing features* • *sense of self* • *memory* • *seeing* • *friendliness* • *imitation*

### Where's the baby?

Do the same as above, but so that your baby moves in and out of view.

### 2-6 months
## *Tummy tickler*

At nappy-changing time blow gently on her tummy. Describe and demonstrate. Repeat – when she giggles do it again.

### 6-12 months
## *Blowing bubbles*

Blow some soap bubbles near to your baby where she can see them. Then encourage her to copy you and to blow the bubbles. You can play a similar game by blowing a feather.

## *The humming game*

Hum a tune and at the same time put your baby's fingers against your lips so that she can feel the vibration. Encourage her to copy you and make the same noise too, "Hmmm...".

# ㊼ Puff and blow

Blowing, whistling or humming on your baby's skin tickles her so you can use any of these techniques to make her **laugh**. But when you get her to copy you, you'll help her develop the muscles used for forming **words**. They make her aware of her **mouth** and what it can do. Combined with sounds you help her make sounds herself with her tongue and lips – a **prelude to talking**.

### Baby skills
that will benefit from "Puff and blow":
• *talking* • *conversation patterns* • *feeling* • *looking* • *listening* • *concentration* • *imitation*

**2** to **12** months  ✓ mind  ✓ talking  moving  hands  ✓ friendliness

# ㊽ Touch and feel

If you gently touch a newborn baby's cheek she'll root around for the nipple to feed. Her skin is highly sensitive and she **responds** immediately to the feeling of **different textures**, especially if they're unfamiliar. Perhaps surprisingly, this can help her develop highly **intellectual skills**, such as the concepts of opposites (rough and smooth, for instance, or hard and soft).

### Baby skills

that will benefit from "Touch and feel":
- *hand control*
- *experimentation*
- *concept of opposites*
- *relaxing* • *anticipation*
- *conversation*

## Understanding opposites

Lay your baby on a play mat on her tummy so that she can feel the textures. Help her stroke opposite textures with her hands – first smooth, then rough. Talk about how each feels.

**Making a touch and feel mat**
There are plenty of baby play mats to choose from in the shops, but you could also make your own by covering a small blanket with a patchwork of squares cut from different textures of material. Stitch them down firmly with wool and make sure there are no loose ends or loops to catch little fingers.

## Touching textures

Give her different fabrics to feel and scrunch, such as satin, towelling and velvet. Later she may use them to initiate games of Peep-bo.

## Exploring a play mat

From three months prop your baby up with cushions or in her baby chair or hold her on your knee. Gather up the play mat and show your baby all the different textures sewn on to the mat. Help her to manipulate them to discover all their different properties.

# What happens next?

Your child's development becomes if anything, more exciting as she enters her second year.

- As she starts walking and talking she begins to **make her mark** as a person.

- Her acquisition of physical, mental and social skills carries on at a **dizzying speed**, but always be realistic and try not to expect too much too soon.

## LOVE AND ENCOURAGEMENT

While she's literally taking her first faltering steps into an adult world and making her first attempts at fitting herself into the family around her, you're her most valued navigator, translator and cheer leader, perhaps the latter being the most important.

Your unconditional acceptance, love and respect are probably the best base for your child to build a healthy self-image. Nothing promotes security, a loving nature, confidence and regard for others like sharing a dignified, loving relationship with you.

The child who has the most confidence is one who accepts herself. This kind of child can cope admirably with the difficulties life throws at her. To keep her happy in the real world it's your job to set her achievable goals so that a sense of failure is never crippling and her self-image remains undamaged.

From time to time it may be necessary to guide her through difficult patches so that she grows up with an understanding of herself and a knowledge of her limitations.

The family environment you create around your child shouldn't limit her opportunities or stifle her curiosity or sense of adventure. If it does, she won't reach her full potential. Encourage her to develop her own individuality rather than trying to fit your child into a set pattern – the pattern you expect. This way you'll teach self-assurance and determination.

Another of your important responsibilities is to teach your child to be aware of others thus ensuring she finds it easy to make friends and avoid the solitary life of a loner. Remember your child will never be accepted socially if anti-social behaviour goes unchallenged.

## TOILET TEACHING

One of the most important areas calling for your good sense and patience is toilet teaching. It's absolutely wrong to expect a child to be dry when you think it's time. The only right time to have such an expectation is when your child is ready.

Ready means that the brain, nerves and muscles are sufficiently well-developed. The nerves are rarely mature or the muscles capable of obeying commands from them before the age of 21 months. So please, for the sake of your child, don't expect results before then. Potty sitting should never be enforced as it will simply make your child refuse to perform and possibly lead to difficulties later.

Accidents are frequent. You'd do well to remember that an 18-month-old barely feels she's passing urine let alone is able to tell you she's going to. In another month she may be able to point or grunt as she wets her nappy, but she can't hold on long enough for you to get her potty. From then on she learns to wait about a minute a week. As she gets older the holding span gets longer till at 2-3 she can hold on for several hours. So the Golden Rules are don't try to "train" early; don't be over-enthusiastic about potties; take your lead from your child and let her go at her own pace; make light of accidents.

## TEACHING INDEPENDENCE

Without a secure feeling of independence a child can't relate to others, share, be reasonable, outgoing and friendly, have a sense of responsibility and eventually respect others and their privacy. Many other qualities stem from her belief in herself – curiosity, adventurousness, being helpful, thoughtful and generous. With such qualities people will relate well to her and she'll automatically get more out of life. What you pour in as love, expresses itself as self-worth and belief in herself. Love of course, is not the only spur; you can encourage her practically as well.

***Helpfulness*** Ask her to fetch things for you – such as the shopping bag or the dustpan – so that she feels useful.

***Decision-making*** Give her small decisions to make – like which toy to play with – so she can use her judgment and rely on it.

***Sense of identity*** Ask questions about her preferences, solicit her opinion to give her a sense of identity and importance.

***Physical independence*** Give her slightly more and more difficult tasks – like jumping up and down, throwing or kicking a ball – so she can feel pleased with the strength and co-ordination of her body.

***Emotional independence*** Show her that she can trust you: you always come back after leaving her, you always comfort her when she's hurt, you always help her when she's in difficulties.

# Index

# Acknowledgments

**Dorling Kindersley would like to thank**

Spencer Holbrook, Elly King, Johnny Pau and Dawn Young for design assistance; Steve Gorton, Gary Ombler, and Andy Crawford for additional photography; Fiona Hunter for proofreading; Hilary Bird for the index.

**Revised edition 2005**

Tomy toys featured in this book are from Dr Miriam Stoppard's Baby Skills Range; fork and spoons on p.82 are from the Always Learning toddler feeding range, developed by Dr Miriam Stoppard and V & A Marketing Ltd.

# baby's
# first skills

**Dr. miriam**
**stoppard**

# Contents